PRISONERS OF FREEDOM

CONTEMPORARY SLOVENIAN POETRY

EDITED BY ALEŠ DEBELJAK

PREFACE BY CHARLES SIMIC

PRISONERS OF FREEDOM

Contemporary Slovenian Poetry

EDITED BY ALEŠ DEBELJAK

With a Preface by Charles Simic

• *p* E D E R N A L •

First edition.

Some of these translations have previously appeared, in slightly different form, in: *Tyuonyi, Matrix, North Atlantic Review, Modern Poetry in Translation, Prism International, Confrontation, Forum, Mundus Artium, Contemporary Literature in Translation, Works: a quarterly of writing; Slovene Studies;* Veno Taufer: *New Music* (University of Tennessee Chapbook Series, Chattanoga, 1990); Dane Zajc: *Ashes* (University of Tennessee Chapbook Series, Chattanooga, 1990); *Contemporary Yugoslav Poetry,* edited by Vasa D. Mihailovich (University of Iowa Press, Iowa City, 1977). Grateful acknowledgement is made to the editors of these publications.

Publication of this book was made possible, in part, by funding from The Pharos Foundation, Impol, United Trade Rep., SK Products, STR Inc., The Rumsey Foundation, the Slovenian Writers' Union, and other individual and private support.

ISBN: 1-881613-00-3

Library of Congress Catalog Card Number: 92-61137

• *p* E D E R N A L •

P.O. Box 23266
Santa Fe, New Mexico 87502 USA

CONTENTS

3

6

7

PRISONERS OF FREEDOM

PREFACE

CHARLES SIMIC

All that really matters about a literature is whether it has good writers or not. Being written in a small language or in a language spoken by millions will determine how many readers and how much influence that literature has, but not its quality. That simple truth came across to me reading this anthology of Slovenian poetry. The number of fine poets Slovenia has had in the last forty years would make proud any literature in the world.

The other question that immediately presents itself concerns the distinctness of the poetry we have here. Is there something uniquely Slovenian about the poets gathered here? This question is much harder to answer today about any literature than it was a hundred years ago. Poets have always been internationalists. They have read and admired each other across cultural borders. In this century, with Modernism, we can even speak of an international style. A poet like Edvard Kocbek shares the historical experience and outlook with many other East European poets. I'm thinking especially of Czeslaw Milosz in Poland and Vladimir Holan in Czechoslovakia. Tomaž Šalamun and Aleš Debeljak could be regarded as a part of the European and American avantgarde. This is to be expected. Like art and the movies, poetry gets around. A young poet in Texas opens a book of Salamun's poems in English, falls in love with them and begins to write like him. Poetry is not what gets lost, but what survives translation. Is there anyone, anywhere who would not be moved by the beauty of this little poem by Milan Jesih?

> A woman pushes
> the heavy chair away from the table, stands up
> tall,
> silent, terrible as an Oriental empire,
>
> and it is
> evening.

Good poetry is both local and universal. The landscape matters, and so do the songs one sings and the bread one eats. "Remember, my child, how mysteriously nature and history are bound together," writes Kocbek. Even more determining is the language one speaks and the stories one tells. "Nations that forget their story-telling," Šalamun writes, "die out." Note the use of folklore in Dane Zajc's "A Crossing:"

First he negotiates it in his dreams.
Rides over it on a white horse.
On a peacock.
On a striped heifer . . . "

Nature, or more precisely country life, is a common subject. Cities like Maribor or Ljubljana do not have the same powerful impact on the imagination of these poets. The lyric poem one encounters in this anthology is usually a nature poem. Beyond that, the poems have a wide range of literary strategies and concerns. The inner life with its psychological nuances and its philosophical questions is also the preoccupation of an unusual number of poems here.

The delights of reading an anthology like this lie in the discovery of poets one has not read before and the poets one has read without realizing their full stature. What a fine lyric poet, for example, Kajetan Kovič is! I was also surprised by Jože Udovič, whose work I knew very little. In the case of Gregor Strniša, his work brought me again the joy, I experienced many years in translating his poems. This brings me to the most important point that needs to be made. We all owe an immense gratitude to the translators here. Without them this anthology would not exist and without the high quality of their work the greatness of Slovenian poetry would have remained a secret.

INTRODUCTION

v

ALEŠ DEBELJAK

THE NATION BORN OF THE SPIRIT OF POETRY

Where is Slovenia? What are the poets like in this *terra incognita* where more than two thousand books are published each year for a tiny nation of two million, and where poetry books are routinely printed in editions of five hundred to three thousand copies?

Textbooks on Central Europe describe it as a small country squeezed between the snow-covered Alps and the warm Adriatic Sea. Forests cover more than fifty percent of Slovenian lands sprinkled with hills, the tops of which are seldom without a typical Baroque church — an indelible mark of central European culture at large. Slovenia's capital, Ljubljana, which received municipal rights in 1220, emerged on the site of the old Roman garrison-camp, Emona, halfway between Vienna and Trieste. These towns were connected by the "southern railway", the lifeline of commercial and cultural life in the Austro-Hungarian empire. In the southern Slovenian lands nestle charming olive plantations on the Mediterranean coast, while to the northeast the country gently sprawls into the Hungarian plains. To the north, the mountain range Karavanke separates it from Austria and from the large Slovenian ethnic minority in the Austrian southernmost region of Carinthia.

During the ten-day war in July 1991, following the public plebiscite and declaration of independence, Slovenia's militiamen sucessfully defended the country against the communist Yugoslav army, thus securing independence for this small country whose population is predominantly Roman Catholic. Had there been no war which dramatically changed the lives of Slovenians and put Slovenia on the map, my American friends would have perhaps known Slovenia only by a few curious items of arcane "Sloveniana". One of them is the vast Carst region in southern Slovenia which enriched scientific imagination with a special terminus technicus, *Protesus anguineus.* The latter describes the beautiful white amphibian, an endemic "human fish" living nowhere else in the world but among the stalagmites in the underground caves of Slovenian Carst. No more familiar than the "human fish" to the

13

uninitiated is a place called Krain in Pennsylvania, named after a medieval city in the heart of Slovenia, or Bahovec Peak in Alaska, named after a pioneer of Slovenian descent. These are but a few examples of the participation of Slovenian emigrants in the colonization of the New World.

In the 19th and 20th centuries, numerous emigrants carrying Italian, Austro-Hungarian, and Yugoslavian passports arrived in America. They had fled from exploitation and foreign domination — a familiar story, indeed. Yet unlike many other emigrant groups, Slovenians left behind an emotional home, though not a political state. In modern times they did not have one. Their hearts must have been full of predictable hope, fear, and anxiety in the face of challenges in the new country — but their suitcases were loaded with books. Instead of contemplating a heroic military tradition and deeds of the sword, historical memories of Slovenians were permeated with deeds of the pen. These memories have kept alive their identity, the foundation of which has been and has remained until today melancholic elegies, lyrical poems of sorrow and grief. The reason for such a commitment to poetry is simple: without political institutions of their own, Slovenians have traditionally looked to poets and writers for moral guidance and spiritual support.

Culture, literature, and language were the pillars of the fragile and tenacious identity of the small nation, both at home and in exile. After World War Two, when the tragic wave of anti-Communist "displaced persons" populated the banks of Ro de la Plata in Argentina, the immigrant community in the endless pampas under the Southern Cross could not make do without books in their mother tongue. Since the Communist blockade prevented them from receiving books from their native country, they have themselves written, translated, and published an impressive number of works including Dante's *Divina Comedia*. One is compelled to say that for Slovenians, even in times of struggle for bare existence, books were as vital for survival as loaves of bread.

Poets and writers were not only priests of language, but also politicians in disguise. In the absence of official political, economic, and cultural institutions, poets and writers took on the role of the *guardians of the mother tongue and individualism, moral independence, and national integrity.* The history of Slovenians is thus not the history of great war victories, but the history of tenacious guerrilla resistance to foreign rulers: literary and linguistic guerrilla resistance, that is. For all practical purposes, Slovenian history is first and foremost spelled out as a history of the Slovenian language, the language which in addition to singular and plural also uses a dual form — one of two world languages that boast of

14

such rarity — which makes it extraordinarily suitable for intimate, personal, and erotic confessions. However, the Slovenian language was forced to assume a more pragmatic role. It continuously had to give voice to ethnic and national sentiments. Due to centuries-long domination by foreigners, mostly Germans, these sentiments were of course more akin to a whisper than to loud cries. National identity, however, remained at the core of the popular imagination bouyed by an unrelenting confidence that the expression of one's national and ethnic identity is a self-evident right. Today, these rights are of course taken for granted; unfortunately, Slovenian history profusely demonstrates that there were few rights Slovenians could have ever taken for granted.

National History, Literary History

Even with a hundred years of independence and sovereignty, the state of Carantania — King Samo's country of Slavs in the seventh century — could not be sustained throughout history. This tradition of sovereignty is now only a nostalgic memory, an illuminating lecture on the glorious past which was surely too short and too remote for its flame to burn until today. Due to past migrations and wars, even the location where the free citizens of the then-prosperous *civitas Carantania* installed their dukes in enthronment rituals no longer lies within the borders of the present state of Slovenia. However, traces of Carantania have survived in more than the mighty stone throne now kept in the museum. The spirit of the first Slovenian state and its democratic procedures is alive and well in important historical records. The ancient ritual for the installation of Carintian dukes, carried out in the Slovenian language, whereby the Slovenian peasants transferred sovereign power to make laws for the community to the dukes, fascinated the celebrated humanist Aeneas Silvius Piccolomini, better known as Pope Pious II. Following his extensive travels to Slovenian lands, he complimented this political ritual as "second to none" in his book *Cosmographia Pii Papae. De Europa* (Paris, 1509). The French legal historian and philosopher Jean Bodin, encouraged by Picolomini's tireless praise, examined the ritual in detail and described it as an original idea for transference of sovereignty that "had no parallel throughout the world". His book *Les Six Livres de la Republique* (1576), where the above praise can be found, remains a classical reference for contractual political theory. Reading Bodin's report on the Slovenian ritual of installation and democratic arrangement between the people and their ruler, Thomas Jefferson was said to have been inspired to write the draft of his *Declaration of Independence.*

15

Yet, even such democratic rules did not help Slovenians to sustain their independence after King Samo's death. Franks, Bavarians, Hungarians, Teutons, and later the Austro-Hungarian Empire became enemies whose belligerent armies advanced towards the warm waters of the Adriatic Sea through the Central European door, setting up political and economic institutions, fighting for money, lands, and souls in the heart of Slovenian country. Nevertheless, Slovenian ethnic islands persisted up to the present day. It is thus a real wonder that Slovenians managed to preserve their specific identity despite and against German, Italian, Hungarian, and Balkan domination. In the absence of a nation-state of their own, the only real home for Slovenians was carved out in their language and poetry. Preservation of national identity had to overcome many political, historical, and social obstacles. Small wonder then that unfavorable circumstances forced many Slovenians to establish their reputation under the aegis of foreign royal courts and patrons.

One of them was Herman de Carinthia, the astronomer, philosopher, translator, and writer, whose philosophical essays were often quoted by Thomas Aquinas' teacher Albertus Magnus. Herman de Carintia participated in the first translation of the Koran from Arabic to Latin in the mid-12th century, in the famous translation workshop of Petrus Venerabilis in the abbey of Cluny. European humanists familiarized themselves for the first time with the Muslim holy book through this translation. Herman's own translation of Ptolemy's *Planispherium* (1143) was the basis for the study of astronomy in Europe for many centuries.

Žiga Herberstein, the diplomat, travel-writer, and cartographer, traveled to Russia several times as an envoy of Maximilian I, the king of Germany and the Holy Roman Empire. Because of Herberstein's expeditions, the entirely unknown Russian lands were introduced to Europe through his scientific work as a cartographer. His knowledge of the Slavic language — his mother tongue having been Slovenian — was instrumental in his scientific efforts. His most important work, *Rerum Moscoviticarum comentarii* (1549) is still frequently reprinted. Its clear narrative, illustrations, descriptions, and maps even today represent a valuable historical source for modern Russian scholars.

In more recent times, another celebrated Slovenian on the Habsburgs' court was Friderik Pregl, the chemist and physicist, who won the Nobel prize for chemistry in 1923.

Among the artists, Jozeph Plečnik, an inventive and extraordinarily talented architect must be singled out. Having finished his training with the famous Viennese architect Oto Wagner, he went to

Prague where he was invited by the president of the pre-war Czech republic, Tomas Masaryk, to design the monumental castle of Hradcani. His original architectural style reflects a genuine reception of classicism and has left its imprint on the facades and structures of many other important monuments across Central Europe. His home town of Ljubljana has been, in architectural terms, almost entirely defined by his original style.

Writers as Spokesmen of the People

Even though written records in Slovenian (sermons, confessions, poems) sporadically appeared from the 10th century on, it was the half century of the Reformation that gave Slovenians a systematic orthography, alphabet, and standardized language. The first book in Slovenian appeared in 1550. Only a few years later Slovenians could read the Old and New Testaments in their mother tongue. Slovenian literature was given birth by Primož Trubar, the Protestant preacher and writer. On the wings of the liberating Reformation movement, which had firmly anchored Slovenian culture into the paradigm of Western civilization, Trubar published his twenty-two books in Germany having fled the religious persecution of Catholic counter-Reformation in his native Slovenia. From Germany he smuggled books to Ljubljana in barrels and carts to be later clandestinely distributed across the Slovenian lands.

It is thus safe to say that writers were the political institutions Slovenians immediately recognized as the true and only authorities. Their artistic work was invested into a single aim: to raise national consciousness. This was anything but easy because theirs was a small nation where the middle class communicated mostly in Italian and German while Slovenian was as a rule reserved for the lower classes, "for peasants and horses", as ironically reported by Edvard Kocbek in his wonderful poem, *Lippizaners.*

Once Roman Catholicism became the dominant religion in the Habsburgs' empire to which Slovenia traditionally belonged, education was given over to the Jesuits. They utilized generous financial support from Archduke Ferdinand and established their college in Ljubljana as early as 1595. This provided the foundation for higher education in the Slovenian lands. The best and brightest Slovenians, however, continued to pursue their advanced studies in traditional Central European centers of learning such as Prague or Cracow, or, for the most part, cosmopolitan Vienna. There they joined ranks with intellectuals from across the Habsburgs' empire.

Later came the short-lived, through productive, French. Four years of Napoleonic rule were followed by the establishment of the Ilyrian Provinces (1809-1813) which stretched along the Adriatic coast all the way to Dubrovnik. For the first time were brought together under one administrative and legislative command two thirds of the ethnic Slovenian territories. This was by no means a small accomplishment. At the same time the French labored hard to institute the Slovenian language in elementary and grammar schools, consequently promoting it as the everyday language of the middle class. Napoleon's regime emphasized the meaning of local languages to an extent inconceivable for the Habsburgs. Slovenian intellectuals and writers thus conveniently familiarized themselves with the French *spirit of the time* which was pregnant with nationalism. The ideas of the French enlightenment were accepted by Slovenians as soon as they appeared while their political, economic, and organizational implementation in the Ilyrian Provinces and its captital, Ljubljana, was immediate.

The first Slovenian poet, Valentin Vodnik (1758-1819), although a Catholic priest, did not write exclusively for religious purposes, but was also devoted to the secrets of everyday life, and it was certainly no accident that he developed his voice under the influences of the Enlightment.

Slovenian national self-consciousness reached its peak in Romanticism. In this respect, it did not lag behind the other Central European peoples that emerged out of "the Spring of Nations". However, relentless pressure on the part of German culture at large and continuous political subjugation from Vienna made it difficult to envision Slovenian survival. Two prominent French travelers, Cyprien Robert and Hyppolite Desprez, were simply recapitulating general colonial impressions when they recorded in 1848, during their travels through Slovenia before and after the "Spring of Nations", that Slovenians would not endure much longer in their resistance to the Germans. Common prediction had it that Slovenians would pass into oblivion as a distinct ethnic community. Stubborn Slovenians, however, proved these speculations wrong. As early as the mid-nineteenth century, Slovenian literary magazines and journals began to be published in Ljubljana that cautiously, yet with increasing attention, tried to come to terms with national and political identity. Having been traditionally denied one, Slovenian writers put the national identity at the core of their work.

The personality and work of France Prešeren (1800-1849), the greatest Slovenian poet, best reveals the longing for freedom and independence. By profession a freeminded lawyer — which is to say, a social outsider — by vocation a Romantic poet of the most ambitious format, he wrote in German, this Central Europen *lingua franca,* as fluently as in Slovenian. Yet for him there was no dilemma: Slovenian was not merely his mother tongue, but the language of choice. It was his article of political faith. In Slovenian he created, in the best Orphean tradition, the everlasting works known by every Slovenian. A genuine Romantic poet of great creative power and drinking habits, Prešeren's private life was underscored by a disillusion. His etheral Laura was a daughter from a respectable bourgeois house, Julia, and in spite of all the beautiful and passionate poems dedicated to her she nevertheless married a German nobleman. Later commentators report, not without musing, that her married life was far from happy. However, what Prešeren did not achieve in his private life he did acomplish on a national level: he failed to win his beloved girl but he succeeded in uniting all Slovenians within one community.

The bloody summer of 1991 saw, in the victorious ten-day war, the poet's creative literature turning into flesh. Slovenians had waited for a long time for their historical dreams to come true. Poetry made their waiting bearable. The June 1991 war literally meant the birth of a Slovenian nation-state from the spirit of poetry.

His poem, *A Toast to Freedom,* is today the Slovenian anthem. But in 1848 the Austrian censors correctly identified its revolutionary potentials in the lyrical metaphors whereby Prešeren called for the union of all Slovenians, if necessary by military resistance to domination:

To whom with acclamation
And song shall we our first toast give?
God save our land and nation
And all Slovenes where'er they live,
Who own the same
Blood and name,
And who one glorious Mother claim.

Let thunder out of heaven
Strike down and smite our wanton foe!

Now, as it once had thriven,
May our dear realm in freedom grow.
May fall the last
Chains of the past
Which bind us still and hold us fast!

Prešeren not only achieved symbolic unification, but also radically redefined Slovenian metaphors, established aesthetic standards, and dramatically pushed the limits of linguistic expression. Each and every person recognized him/herself in the poetic description of the universal human condition, carrying the message of the Romantic idea about freedom and peace as something that holds true not only for one nation but for all people:

God's blessing on all nations,
Who long and work for that bright day,
When o'er earth's habitations
No war, no strife shall hold its sway;
Who long to see
That all men free
No more shall foes, but neighbors be.
— *A Toast to Freedom,* translated by Janko Lavrin

Prešeren's poetry accomplished something of a miracle. With the poems in which national and individual destiny blend into one universal message about liberation, Prešeren managed to rekindle the subdued flame of national self-consciousness. As demonstrated, Slovenians had nothing else that could stand for a firm unifyng bond except their language. It took the poet to turn language from a means of expression into the foundation of national substance as well as the manifestation of national identity. It is no surprise then that Slovenians are so sensitive about their language.

After the disintegration of the Austro-Hungarian Empire and in the wake of the First World War, a greater freedom was sought in the new common state of the Southern Slavs, called the *Kingdom of Serbs, Croats, and Slovenians,* and later renamed, Yugoslavia. At first glace the new state appeared an ideal solution for the small Slovenian nation. In 1919 Slovenian became the language of instruction at the newly established University of Ljubljana. Slovenians could finally use their national idiom without restrictions. Accordingly, they committed themselves to cultural life with extraordinary vigor, enthusiasm, and creative drive. Slovenian-American writer Louis Adamic who sailed to the American shores in his boyhood, and later befriended Upton Sinclair, went on to write a number of realistic novels and short stories in English. In one of them he described his home country during a visit before the Second World War:

"Gradually I realized what I had dimly known in my boyhood, that, next to agriculture, Slovenia's leading industry was Culture. In Lublyana were seven large bookshops (as large as most of the hardware, drygoods, and drugstores in town), two of them more than a hundred years old . . . Besides, each bookstore carried a selection of the latest German, French, Czech, Serbo-Croat, English and Italian books . . . In Slovenia nearly everybody — merchants, peasants, priests, teachers, students — bought books anyhow . . . In two years there had been forty-eight performances of Hamlet in Lublyana. Most of the city's streets are named after poets, essayists, novelists, dramatists, grammarians. The largest monument in town is to the poet, France Presheren . . . When students take hikes into the country, their destinations usually are the graves and birthplaces of poets, dramatists, and other writers."
— *The Native's Return,* Louis Adamic (1934)

Louis Adamic's perspective is correct though not complete. The situation was by no means as idyllic as it appeared to the sentimental visitor who was keen to see only the flattering aspects of life in the land of his youth.

The truth is that after the Second World War a significant number of Slovenians found themselves in Italy. As much as one third of Slovenians had to become, by hook or by crook, Italian citizens. Their scorned Slovenian descent made them second-rate citizens in Mussolini's state. Slovenians came under strong Fascist pressure: their press was prohibited, their schools were closed, priests could only hold illegal masses in clandestine locations. Many emigrated, but many more continued their struggle for national and cultural freedom, for the freedom to speak their language.

The importance of Mediterranean Slovenian life is demonstrated by the fact that it was not the landlocked Ljubljana but Trieste — a cosmopolitan Adriatic port which, in 1918, was one of the biggest Slovenian towns besides Ljubljana and Cleveland, Ohio — where Slovenians planned to establish their university. It would not have lasted long. The situation was indeed dramatic: public use of Slovenian subjected those who dared to challenge the Fascist-imposed hegemony of Italian to high fines and imprisonment. Slovenian teachers were exiled by force, brutal right-wing squads burned to the ground the Slovenian National House, the principal Slovenian cultural institution in the heart of Trieste. The Fascist battle cry, "eia eia alala" eerily echoed throughout Slovenian neighborhoods, and Slovenian nationalists were being killed. Trieste might have made a pleasant retreat for a talented writer in search of the eternal "there". James Joyce, a Trieste college teacher, enjoyed a cozy atmosphere there. For Slovenians, alas, Trieste represented a linguistic and cultural straight-jacket. While Italians and Austrians were charmed by Trieste's numerous cafes, promenades, and well-mannered aristocratic circles, Slovenian experience speaks of an oppresive place, an internal exile, with a rising tide of violence, a true "heart of darkness" which has been conveniently overlooked in the recent debates on Central Europe.

At the same time in the southern Austrian region of Carinthia, the site of the first independent Slovenian state, increasingly aggressive Nazi thugs in notorious brown shirts terrorized Slovenian people, vandalized their homes, and beat Slovenian students and peasants. The former capital of the empire, Vienna, was in geographical terms little more than three hundred miles away; in terms of the human and national rights of the Slovenian minority, it could have been on another planet.

Outside Austria the situation was not much more encouraging. Slovenian heart-felt hopes were invested in the union with their "brethern", south Slavs. The union was believed to bring political and economic protection and enable them to start a fully-developed national life. Their hopes soon collapsed. Serbian, the language of the royal court and the most populous nation, became the language of public and official communication. High officials of centralized state institutions as a rule came from Belgrade, more than five hundred miles away from Ljubljana. The Slovenian language was put to the Procrustean bed of the Cyrillic alphabet and was denied its genuine Latin alphabet. Slovenian intellectuals were routinely appointed to posts in the heart of Bosnia, Serbia, and Montenegro. Slovenian became a second-rate language. Later the Belgrade regime, which since 1929 had resorted to open dictatorship, tried to eradicate Slovenian identity on a nominal level as well. It arranged for Slovenia to comprise, with western Croatian districts, a bogus province without a distinct name.

In spite of repeated historical deception, Slovenian persistence did not relax. Vibrant literary life reflected the aesthetic trends of Paris and Vienna, pale-faced young men recited their rebellious poems in clubs and coffee houses, literary debates on expressionism, constructivism, and surrealism were imbued with political overtones. The uneasy bond between politics and literature became a question of life and death after the Nazi invasion of Yugoslavia in 1941.

Prešeren's poetic idea that it is better to die than to be a slave once again provided moral, existential, and national guidance. Most writers joined partisans and fled to the woods where, in the midst of the raging war, they printed their books, newspapers, and magazines in makeshift printshops. In temporarily-liberated areas they organized literary readings, published reviews, and vigorously encouraged people to resist occupation. Needless to emphasize, many of them died for freedom while writing and fighting, writing in the fight.

Contemporary Ljubljana is perhaps the only European capital where a visitor can look in vain for the monuments of generals and victorious cavalrymen. Despite the liberation war and the revolution, Slovenians continue to be more attracted by the pen than the sword. Instead of generals, Slovenians placed on privileged pedestals their poets. As noted by Louis Adamic, many streets are named after celebrated masters of the pen, their faces solemnly gazing from new banknotes. During the Second World War many Slovenian partisan brigades were named after poets and writers, which is another historically rare example of the vital importance of literature to this small nation.

After the war, many writers entered government administration. A renowned prewar poet, partisan, and Christian Socialist, Edvard Kocbek, became vice-president of the Slovenian government and a minister in the federal Yugoslav government. He remained there until he fell out of favor due to his refusal to give up his literary mission. His poems, stories, and journals bear witness to his courage to criticize his former colleagues' black-and-white dramaturgy that characterized communist aesthetics. Edvard Kocbek's was the poetic pursuit of truth and the fight for freedom that guards language against authoritarian newspeak. Kocbek was also the first to daresay the carefully-guarded communist secret in public: the liberation war was, to a considerable degree, a civil war between the "reds" and the "whites". The poet won over the statesman. Kocbek thus remained indebted to the legacy of Preseren: only after having lost direct access to the mechanisms of power and having become a dropout and a dissident, was he able to tell the bitter truth, the full truth.

Poetry and Dissent

Even though Edvard Kocbek was widely acclaimed, no fame helped him escape the fate of an internal exile which denied him publishing opportunities and public contact with his readership. However, the seeds of resistance to the communist regime had been planted. Jože Udovič, himself a veteran of partisan resistance and a highly esteemed senior poet, wrote before the war although most of this work saw publication only after the war. Yet, he wrote his poems in an almost pathological isolation from readers and critics alike. This was a direct result of his disillusion with the communist politics of deception. He rejected all awards, did not appear at official functions, and declined interviews. Such was his way of saying, *No, thank you!* to political intrusions. In his poems, however, he created a moving world of gradual disintegration of romantic subjects and a retreat from the ideal of beauty. The latter remained an idealized Ithaca even though the poet was aware that it was only a "mirror of dreams".

The Yugoslav political break with Moscow in 1948 spelled the end of aesthetically and ethically worthless poetry which submissively celebrated revolutionary accomplishments. 1953 saw the publication of the first book of lyrical poems that stood head and shoulders above the then-obligatory social-realistic aesthetics. Of the poets who rehabilitated deeply personal voices in the tiny volume, *Poems of Four Poets*, Kajetan Kovič commanded the most respect. His was an original vision of darkness and bitterness that drew upon two sources: resigned yet not desperate confrontation with death as a legacy of the war generation, and an Orphean motif that gave credence to the poet as a voice of historical truth and redemption.

The late fifties and the early sixties were periods of literary eruption. New independent journals were established, spearheaded by the most radical such as *Beseda* (The Word), *Revija 57* (Review 57), and *Perspective* (Perspectives). The first poetry books by Dane Zajc and Veno Taufer appeared in private editions because of obstruction by the

24

authorities. Despite roadblocks, poetry continued to gain more freedom. The vision of death and metaphysical void as a wartime legacy were given existentialist and absurdist grounding in the generation of repression-savvy poets like Dane Zajc, Veno Taufer, and Gregor Strniša.

The mythological poetry of Gregor Strniša elevated the modern imagination of his time to the point where heaven meets hell. The world was perceived as a kingdom of dark, cruel, and mysterious forces. It was embedded in the aesthetic narrative of cold description replete with mythical creatures and fairy tales.

Strniša's poems point out two relevant things. First, everyday life is the greatest mystery and second, loneliness is not just the absence of others, but a life among people who do not understand what you are saying. This was an excellent poetic definition of the historical condition of the Slovenians as a people.

Svetlana Makarovič would later proceed along the same lines. In her own style she recreated an atmosphere of folk songs, traditionally melancholic and full of longing for something that is lost forever.

Social reality by all means buttressed such dark visions. The red horizons of postwar optimism turned in the early sixties into faded photographs from an historical album. Heaven had not descended to earth, happiness and progress asserted their presence only in official rhetoric. The pursuit of truth was carried out in poetry books.

The secret agents of the regime, "experts of metaphors", knew that poets enjoyed alarmingly wide support among the common people. Literary magazines, those strongholds of writers and independent intellectuals, published increasingly biting criticism of corruption and political impasse. This process of growing dissent culminated in 1964 in massive popular protests.

Many attended literary gatherings, campuses were boiling, night after night poets read their works to enthusiastic audiences of students. They demanded change. The panic-stricken authorities organized duped workers to protest against artists and intellectuals during theater performances which ridiculed leading politicians. Communist apparatchiks must pinpoint a victim. They arrested Tomaž Šalamun, a leading young poet who blasphemously rewrote canonized patriotic poems and called into question the hypocrisy of the regime. His most threatening quality seemed to be the fact that the party-line education which was systematically invested into the resigned population completely failed with Šalamun: equipped with his talent for poetic absurdity, irony, and radical playfulness he proclaimed, not unlike his spiritual godfather Arthur Rimbaud, that all dogmatic tradition is the "game of countless idiotic generations".

The leading cultural magazine, *Perspectives,* was first censored and then suspended. In the realm of Slovenian culture the year 1964 and the far-reaching consequences of civil disobedience and political dissent not only represents a harbinger of the May of 1968, but gives shape to the dissident imagination in decades to come.

Between Solidarity and Solitude

The dissenting year of 1964 is followed by an era of renewed Stalinist repression which runs strongly until the early eighties. Intellectuals and writers were silenced or exiled. A short intermezzo in 1971, when students occupied the University for several weeks, was not long enough to recharge the batteries of moral revolt. After the students' defeat, a retreat into the intimate world seemed to be the only solution. The poets baptised by fire during the occupation of the University, notably Boris A. Novak, Milan Dekleva, and Milan Jesih (who was brought to court because of his active participation in protest literary readings), have the taste of defeat inscribed on their hearts. Censorship became stricter, many writers could not publish, few were employed, social marginalization was their home. Poets, however, did not forget that "if you do not deal with politics, politics deals with you" as shrewdly put by Czech philosopher Karel Kosik. Instead of conforming to the standards of social life, poets continued to whisper of a world inside their minds, singing true songs to "the minimal self". Alienation from external reality inevitably lead them to rediscover language as the house of being, as Heidegger would have it.

They explored the limits of lyrical technique, the depths of metaphor, strategies of verse-formation, and foreign cultures, as exemplified by Ivo Svetina. In his work, prudence and sadness move from the contents into the design of the poem, while irony, the cult of beauty, and poetic wise-cracking are employed as a protection against, not as a challenge to, external reality. The poet's solitude became a central moral principle: resistance is passively expressed through non-involvement in the officially-dictated cultural and political life.

After ten years of poetic retreat, public repression, and closed public space the intellectuals' patience wore thin. The early eighties saw the launching of a new magazine whose very name reveals the manner in which it tried to open public debate: *Nova revija* (The New Review). Not incidentally, several ministers of the independent state in 1991 were recruited out of the group of dissident writers and human rights activists around this important cultural review. Poets of the seventies, having traveled all the way from harmless linguistic "exercises in style" to the depths of existence and moral need for "life in truth", joined this circle. From the former dwellers of the ivory towers of textuality, they turned into actors in the "arena of life". Many, notably the leading formalist poet Boris A. Novak, became radically involved in civil disobedience through such socially marginal, yet morally potent, organizations as the Writers Union and P.E.N. Center.

The poems, novels, testimonies, and short stories that writers managed to publish, despite censorship, gradually peeled off layers of lies: the truth about the horrors of Stalinism, about *The Naked Island* — the Yugoslav Gulag that swallowed many dissidents, regime opponents, and writers — was finally made public. The writers were again at the fore. The communist regime gradually lost ground. In the late eighties, writers joined forces with sociologists to challenge the system by writing a proposal for a new constitution. In keeping with honored tradition, the writers acted instead on behalf of the politicians.

In the larger frame of Yugoslavia, growing Serbian appetites in the late eighties represented a tangible threat to the other Yugoslav nations: Serbs usurped the federal administration, illegally appropriated more than half of the hard currency reserves of the federal bank, and Kosovo experiences the imposition of apartheid on ethnic Albanians. Even a blind man could see that Slovenia had to choose between two alternatives: remain under the heel of corrupted communist authorities in Belgarde who openly flexed their muscles, or establish an independent state.

Historical responsibility inspired writers to hammer out a draft of the new constitution by which they masterfully challenged the communists' grip on power. It was again writers who pushed popular revolt past the point of no return. Following heated public debates, writers and poets lead a group of dissidents and members of the democratic opposition into drafting up no less than the declaration of Slovenian independence. It won immediate support in the public at large. Stimulated by such actions even Slovenian communists mustered enough political instinct and courage to resist the centralist government. After a public referendum demonstrated by overwhelming margin the wish of the Slovenian people to live in a free Slovenia, the independent state was declared. Poets, writers, and their readers celebrated.

By the end of the eighties, pressing political and state-building concerns by and large ceased to necessitate the use of Aesopian language and cryptic poetic metaphors. These conditions in particular appealed to the poets that came of age in the eighties. While older colleagues spearheaded the struggle for an independent state, the nascent generation felt somewhat left aside: hence their inclination to explore the formal and metaphysical possibilities of poetic imagination and their refusal to view literature as the one and only platform from which political opinions could be voiced. However, the separation of politics and literature, these often strange bedfellows, was never meant to give birth to some myopic version of *l'art pour l'art.* Insofar as moral habits are embedded in the intricacies of historic allegory and allusion, the unfettered urge to stress them expressively is beside the point, argued young Slovenian poets. *The poet's task to recognize history and its discontents is always present,* as their lyrical poems clearly demonstrated. The poet's historical sensibility makes its way into the poem by virtue of language, a shared stock of metaphors, and cultural tradition.

Arguing for a critical separation of civil engagement on the one hand, and autonomous writing on the other — long overdue in Central and Eastern Europe as a whole — the young poets championed a distinct attitude: a writer can only aspire to be a witness of his or her times if the writing itself is free of any external prescriptions. The young poets hence espoused a kind of Joycean *non seviam* to the cause of Slovenian independence. I shall haste to add that their civic and moral responsibility was, in keeping with the best Slovenian tradition of intellectuals *qua* politicians, articulated outside the literary medium, notably in newspaper columns and other public forums. This was a novel approach to poetry in the Central and Eastern Europe customarily associated with a noble mind which is, as Czeslaw Milosz once remarked, of no particular use for literature. From this vantage point one can see that young Slovenian poets believed a creative self can only bloom beyond the divisions of progressive *vs* conservative. A writer may only aspire to be a witness of his/her times if the writing itself is free of any external prescriptions, regardless of the political cause.

The views of the young poets aptly corresponded with the radically changed cultural situation in the independent state. The writers' historical mission is for the most part accomplished. Slovenians now have a nation-state. Prešeren's toast to freedom may now be sung in a free country, not clandestinely but at official functions and, if one wishes, at the top of one's lungs. New social and historical conditions care predictably less for poems and more for business, advancing the commerce of goods rather than the commerce of ideas. Literature in this social context *no longer represents the privileged forum of truth, justice, and beauty* and thus, by extension, of national identity. The role of the poet as a revered *shaman* and *people's spokesman* who tells the stories about historical taboos, repressed memory, about individual solitude and social resistance, is in all likelihood over. The curtains are being drawn, the performance of writers as decisive actors in the public arena is slowly coming to an end.

The social meaning of the writer's vocation has irreversibly *changed.* If the writer no longer runs the risk of going to prison for what he publishes, then his word lacks the moral weight it carried before. As long as the writers' search for an answer to the question about *ex Oriente lus,* "the light from the East", is answered in a reader's happy singing about craving for *ex Occidente luxus,* "luxurious goods from the West", the writers have only one chance left. Writers need to abandon the endless discussions about socialism with a human face and its radical criticism. Rather, they need to focus on the human face alone. In other words, a political theme no longer provides a desired historical and aesthetic alibi.

This important insight is now being widely accepted by Slovenian writers. Such consensus is no small accomplishment. Inasmuch as a free man does not inquire about his freedom, contemporary Slovenian poetry, pregnant with historical memories of repression, thus puts itself on the best path to become a free expression of free men and women.

EDVARD KOCBEK

THE LIPPIZANERS

A newspaper reports:
the Lippizaners collaborated
on an historical film.
A radio explains:
a millionaire had bought the Lippizaners,
the noble animals were quiet
throughout the journey over the Atlantic.
And a textbook teaches:
the Lippizaners are graceful riding horses,
their origin is in the Karst, they are of supple hoof,
conceited trot, intelligent nature
and obstinate fidelity.

But I have to add, my son,
that it isn't possible to fit these
restless animals into any set pattern:
it is good, when the day shines,
the Lippizaners are black foals.
And it is good, when the night reigns,
the Lippizaners are white mares,
but the best is,
when the day comes out of the night,
then the Lippizaners are white and black buffoons,
the court fools of its Majesty,
Slovene history.

Others have worshipped holy cows and dragons,
thousand-year old turtles and winged lions,
unicorns, double-headed eagles and phoenixes,

but we've chosen the most beautiful animal,
which proved to be excellent on battlefields, in circuses,
harnessed to princesses and the Golden Monstrance,
therefore the emperors of Vienna spoke
French with skillful diplomats,
Italian with charming actresses,
Spanish with the infinite God,
and German with uneducated servants:
but with the horses they talked Slovene.

Remember, my child, how mysteriously
nature and history are bound together,
and how different are the driving forces of the spirit
of each of the world's peoples.
You know well that ours is the land of contests and races.
You, thus, understand, why the white horses
from Noah's ark found a refuge on our pure ground,
why they became our holy animal,
why they entered into the legend of history,
and why they bring the life pulse to our future.
They incessantly search for our promised land
and are becoming our spirit's passionate saddle.

I endlessly sit on a black and white horse,
my beloved son,
like a Bedouin chieftain
I blend with my animal,
I've been traveling on it all my life,
I sleep on it, and I dream on it
and I'll die on it.
I learned all our prophesies
on that mysterious animal,
and this poem, too, I experienced
on its trembling back.

Nothing is darker than
clear speech,
and nothing more true than a poem,
which the intellect cannot seize,
heroes limp in the bright sun,
and sages stammer in the dark,

the buffoons, though, are changing into poets,
the winged Pegasi run faster and faster
above the caves of our old earth
jumping and pounding —
the impatient Slovene animals
are still trying to awaken King Matjaž.

Those who don't know how to ride a horse
should learn quickly
how to tame the fiery animal,
how to ride freely in a light saddle,
how to catch the harmony of the trot,
and above all to persist in the premonition,
for our horses came galloping from far away,
and they still have far to go:
motors tend to break down,
elephants eat too much,
our road is a long one,
and it is too far to walk.

MOUNTAIN

Whenever I look at you, you are magnificent
and when I gaze at your peak from nearby
my lips start to tremble, whispering, oh sacred
mountain, oh solemn and mysterious mountain, oh
untamed and maternal mountain, oh
the primal and bold flight toward the sky
full of sighs and venerable memories
oh dreaming mountain, locked within yourself
with myriads of scars. You seem indifferent
to your secrecy, but in truth your serenity
terrifies me, though I can never see you from all sides.
In silence I hear the purity of your memories,
sense your eternal walk toward home
and knowing you'll reach it
your calm assurance is ancient.
You force a man who looks upon you
to doubt himself, discovering your
true secret: you are the most magnificent pregnant woman,

shyly close to giving birth,
shifting imperceptibly in choosing the beautiful green dress
with white and blue flowers,
you are on your way to the secret place
the volcanic breath has awakened in you
your breathing agitates the wild animals and tells of
the widening of your womb,
your breasts are swelling with divine milk
and wild honey,
the clouds above you tell the story of your
indestructible mythology
they all want to be a part of the celebration
of you giving birth
and I, too, am in awe, am repeating
the words of glory: oh magnificent mountain,
oh wild mountain, oh sacred and solemn mountain,
the maternal, the mysterious.

LESSER PSALM

I sing a song to duration, giving solid ground under me,
that I can lean on when I pause.
I sing a song to the invulnerable soul of the world, it always
bounces back, forgetting its fear, again and again untamed.
I sing a song to the inexhaustible depths of existence, the more
solitary daring is, the more noble the weariness.
I sing a song to seeds, pulsating evenly always, opening and
closing, offering their secret jealousy.
I sing a song to the playfulness of the spirit, repeating
itself in always new circles, rising from blurry labyrinths,
awaiting an appearance in the soft tissue.
I sing a song to gifts, visiting us again and again, one gift
surprised at the other, all movingly ignorant.
I sing a song to the always-new truth, loving us as a virgin
bride, we follow it, and are never able to catch up with it.
I sing a song to the incomprehensible, making us anxious and
passionate, and to the beatitude, opening in it softly.
I sing a song to the finite, to this melancholic sister, standing
on the edge of the world, curiously tranquil and docile.
I sing a song of waiting, bending inside us like ripened wheat,

silence is closest to maturity.
I sing a song to movement, it challenges us to face the
unknown.
I sing a song to suffering, renewing us, we change in spasms
as crackling wood in fire.
I sing a song to pain, destroying the heart, blood drips on
earth, superhumanhood bends its head.
I sing a song to bliss, in its tranquil completeness we don't
know what more to do, embraced and fed by a mystical suppleness.
I sing a song to joy, always abundant, we chatter happily and
move enthusiastically, man is a consolable child.
I sing a song to love, at last, singing a warm song that I will
never again forget.

SLOVENIAN HYMN

Small and meek, I grow into the cosmic order, my brothers speak
the same words as I, lifted from idleness, we
gaze at the sphere of the earth.
The earth has been neatly drawn, the ground is indomitable, we
set up our white houses long ago and bordered
them in blue.
Its furrowed surface is worked into a wistful sky, live dark
belts encircle it, all measures have banded
wisely together.
Streams purl over the earth and springs gurgle, forests
saturate, fields sprawl in tacit persistence,
flies swarm in the sunlight, gnats over twilight
paths.
From village to village it is neither too far nor too near,
enclosed gardens surround the homesteads, a dark
green hedge looks out over a fence.
Fruit trees ripen around the houses, the wind prowls in their
branches, a steep trail leads up to the vineyards,
down to the cellar where mallet blows thud dully.
Huge wardrobes stand in the parlors, the wall clock's pendulum
chats with eternity, a cat kneads by the oven,
and apricot trees blossom in the soft grass
below the fields.
The sun illuminates the great altar at evening, mass and the

people's singing blends with incense, while now
and then a schoolboy drops his hat.
Girls wear white kerchiefs to vespers, a flower pressed in the
prayer book of each, and during the way of the
cross they glance at the acolytes in black.
Pigeons cluck in the graveyard chapel, bats hang in the church
tower, bees have their hive by the stream and
mushrooms grow in places only old wives know.
Modest plum and apple trees flower in fertile ground, grain
billows over gentle hillsides and flatlands,
an occasional fish leaps out of the frothy water.
Fields of dry gold lie benumbed in the summer heat, shepherds
light fires in high autumn meadows, a song about
vineyards resounds amid strokes of mallets.
We dance at banquets and listen to a comical fiddler, and as we
sort through seeds by the warm stove the wind and
a creaky wagon strapped with chains go past
together.
Experience dozes on the hay and in forests, love stirs in
distracted young boys, candles burn at graves
and bells chime at midnight mass.
The holidays range from All Souls to Corpus Christi and Marymas,
buckwheat follows wheat, turnips barley,
we set out potatoes in the fallows, clover grows
wild among the wheat.
People are like ants in the fields and on hillsides, at times a
voice calls from the distance, which another one
answers.
Asleep, there is a flicker of the thought of work, during work
hope smolders, hope is tinged with sadness, then
churchbells ring again.
Lifted from our idleness we gaze at the earth's sphere, and lo,
the more deeply we stare, the heavier the deepness,
stunned with pain we taste the bitterness of roots.
And look, smoke sweeps the horizon, swallows look
plaintively from their nests, a bronze bell has
cracked down the middle.
In silence mothers rock their children, potters' wheels stop,
fabric rips on the loom, day laborers have bent their
backs for years.
O land of our fathers, given to us like an enchanted princess,

when will you be saved?
You are our night phantom, our morning burden, midday muddle and
        evening sadness, holy redemption wells up within us.
Disowned, you endure, great mother, quietly calling us, you have
        been ravaged, fertile body, and your children put to shame.
Our footsteps cry out to you, our kinship and comfort, we lift up
        our hands from your ancient soil and answer.
At night your eyes open like a passionflower, you take count of
        us, beside your hearth our souls beat as one.
You are the ark of our covenant, which we guard, we must be
        watchful each night and sing the songs we are
        pledged to.
O fearsome ripening of the ageless secret, unspeakably strong
        wine, we sense you in our blood, we are drunk
        like young fathers.

FIERY NIGHT

On the night before Easter Sunday
atop the Pannonnian hills we set
pitchy bonfires and kept watch
to see which blaze would be strongest.
Wreathes of flame shot into the sky
and climaxed in fulgent haloes.
We jumped through the bonfires and sang,
weird shadows crouching behind us.

Tonight darkness rekindles the fires.
The old shadows return
to oppress us vengefully,
the alien gods burn with fury.
Torchlike arrows rip the sky,
drums rumble, horns blare,
fakirs with frothing mouths dance.
My farewell to the world has begun.

The ring around me pulls tighter and tighter,
its teeth join in a blazing pyre.
Earth raises me onto a column
high above the fiery sea.

I looked for glory and I found it.
This night is great, this night is mine,
whether I burn and am saved
or remain and stammer to my death.

IN A TORCHED VILLAGE

I lean on a wall
still hot
from the long fire,
nowhere a villager,
nowhere a villain,
the ground gives way,
the universe sways
stars perish.

There is a surge, suddenly,
of the scent of violets.
I begin to hear
gentle voices:
grass rising
for new footsteps,
ashes cohering
to a new strength.

A spring gushes into
its stone trough,
a cat returns
to its scorched doorstone.
I grow more and more,
become a giant,
now I see over
the horror's shoulders.

WHO AM I?

I never am
what people think I am,
and never where

eyes see me.
Enemies say that I'm
the heir apparent,
my friends maintain that I'm
a covert monk,
and wags would have me
rotting in the ship's log
of a sunken vessel
that sought new lands.
But I kneel down at noon
and etch dictations of silence
in the desert sand,
toward evening gnash my teeth
in a dangerous crevice
of the tower of Babel,
and at night lie meekly down
among the swords
on Hamlet's terrace.
Only toward morning
do I swing up in the horizon's saddle
at the farthest corner of the world
and set out to find
the generous rose
ready to erupt.
One day it will look
this arrogant century in the face
and the century will blush.

PONTUS

Where I am is the Pontus.
The Pontus is exile.
Exile is reminiscent of paradise,
though I can't remember it.
My enemy's power has faded,
no longer summons me with passion,
no longer returns me to my self.

I walk over mountains and fields,
open books and look at birds

and seek my opposite.
I call to it and long for it
to unsettle me violently.
But exile is freedom
with no opponent, no confrontation.

LANDSCAPE

The spirit of wild animals
approaches the houses,
pregnant women
move their lips,
the ripe space smells
of some greasy substance
and hollow grain.
Fruit has fed the worms,
flowers returned
to their beehive,
the landscape retreats
from its outlines.
Silence archaically rattles,
memory weighs anchor,
moonlight toys with
a peacock's tail.
Things grow bigger
than their presence,
drunks can't get enough of thirst,
or animals to the bottom
of their innocence.
The wind feeds on fissures,
darkness on thieves.
The world is riddled
with longing aches.
I turn within a circle
as in wedding dreams,
unable to recall
the right incantation.

SMUGGLING

There is no clear crossing anymore —
carefully marked
and fatefully sensed,
nothing jabs at your heel
or heart now
as you walk through the minefield,
the border is hidden,
there is only a quiet mingling,
a gradual transition,
a slow loss of ease,
an expansion of ill,
a pulling on of gloves,
opening of umbrellas,
a calling for help,
a mixing of inward
and outward darkness,
victim and perpetrator
secretly join,
two pristine peaks and between them
a swampy valley thickly overgrown,
one Achilles among countless others like him.
The smuggling is en masse,
the border guard has stopped
inspecting and keeps low.
Now he just takes pleasure in
the covert crossing.

STRAIGHT LINE

The famous painter abruptly drew
a straight line and knew that he was dying,
because all his life he had tried
to draw a straight line but
had never managed. Although his spirit always
strained, birds would describe playful
arcs around him and distract
his hand. So he lay down and coolly

wondered, What is talent? And what
is human freedom? He was aware his
grandson knew the epact and discovered comets,
but he had realized only now that there
was no straight line at all, since all our life
is crooked. Look, even sleep is a magical
bending of wakefulness.
And so it is much later than time would indicate,
and each flower constantly grows heavier, the universe
more curved.

OCCURENCE

The same thing keeps recurring:
a twitching that I cannot subdue.
From time to time a rhythmical crackling,
as of wood settling thoughout the house.
At night and by day an easing of tension,
first in the furniture, then in the floor,
in the wall somewhere, the light fixture, my books.
Each time some place new, each time inevitable,
as though building toward an earthquake or
as though a treacherous power were mounting
and the house might collapse, or somebody
immured in the wall would knock and
step through it at any minute. I swallow
with difficulty, ensnared in creaking.
I sense it acutely and I know: the warm silence
of things, the horrible aloneness of primeval,
wearisome matter. Even now the ocean washes over
England. Even now glowing magma settles
beneath our feet. In the dark I decipher the unknown writing
on the wall. In the dark I see huge eyes,
and in dreams a horrible land of whirlwinds.

AUGUST'S SOLITUDE

When his foes had slowly
shucked him, heavy rose,
and with nakedness obscured him,
he took refuge in the arcane rapture
seeds and herbs have
in the attic of an afternoon,
and much like a sorcerer,
with belief unbounded in a secret knowledge
lifted off into the air
to remain there at the end of a rope,
fulfilled and upstanding
among the good tools and the worn-out objects
among the calendars and almanacs
and the Black Book of the farmer's calling,
becalmed, touchingly true,
illuminated beyond his mind,
by suffering blessed,
and so a part of things
that at midnight, anew,
he'll touch his father's floor,
doff the martyr's wreath, and,
returned to sacred cares,
will begin walking about the house,
will step into the yard,
yoke the remaining horse to the plough
and ride off to the clearing in the moonlight
to finish up in the fields
they took from him years ago
and which even now lie fallow.

LONGING FOR PRISON

I missed the most important
spiritual retreat of my life,
I am left without proof
of my true worth,
every prison is a treasury,

a secret compartment, a jealous
torture house, the most important stage
of the executioner's asceticism, just before
a naked woman, a knife in her hand, corrupts him,
I missed the delight of this love,
for I would die more easily had I
counted the squares on the floor of solitary
and conjured up transparent frescoes
on the dusty window, and
gazed from time to time
at the frontier outposts of humanity.
You have collapsed now, cell,
disintegrated into openness,
the world's no longer cruelty redemptive,
it's only a courtyard on a Saturday afternoon.
Now you can no longer test me,
I am no longer a figurine for a creche,
for puppetry, or a robot performance.
I am preparing for a different game,
look, I'm turning into a gray little mouse,
I have only the smallest hiding places,
tonight I'll weather in the empty sleeve of a child
with no right arm, tomorrow I'll dream
in the echo of a shadow asleep after its journey
through a fairy tale with no end.
I can say to the words deliverance and comfort,
the words toy and grace are choking me,
landing on my eyes are those shot as they fled,
man, mother, love, loyalty,
on my breast lie down the unhappy ones
which I neglected or never pronounced,
and one among them nests
right in my trembling lips,
never have I seen it in the lexicon.

JOŽE UDOVIČ

LEADEN, SLANTING RAIN

The lightly rigged skiff
has foundered.
You haven't discovered the coast
which the morning winds promised.
In the hot sand not a trace
of Odysseus's footsteps.
No sign of an oracle,
column-unclosed,
at the foot of youth's volcano.
The sibyl is silent.

The white, translucent statue
did not glow like a miracle.
In its draperies' folds
ossified time seemed lusterless, gray,
and its cold marble eyes
stared at you, senseless.

Nor did you care to try
the lotus flower, the fruit of forgetting,
in lands not a revelation.
A river flowed slowly:
beyond lay a brown, scorched desert,
here, cliffs and turbid water
littered with dry leaves.

Toward evening you said,
"Boatsman, take me across,
past the reefs of this dark hour,
they harbour a chasm,
a watery path to

the underworld's shores."

And he set out, rowing
toward the old, familiar coastline.
In the distance he saw it:
bare trees, a low horizon
and falling on these a leaden,
slanting rain.

LITTLE NIGHT MUSIC

Stars, the sky's crickets,
sang in night's meadow; as it approached,
it passed a burning bush,
its footsteps echoing
in the valley of the moon.

It came in clothing
woven from fragile birdsong,
and in the wind's cut-glass shoes.

And it lit candles,
changed one to a child,
a traveler, a gardener;
a white windmill clanked in its voice,
its eyes were dark
saffron with gold powder,
and its heart
a diving swallow.

THE BOAT

Let me stay
this night far out,
alone upon the swelling wave,
upon the wave that changes darkly
everything that breathes.
And in the boat of change
I'll play, in the boat of desire

carrying it off,
on the wave of shadow, which is cold,
on the reflection which weaves at night
long wreathes
and hangs them on the marked man's
neck. Let me stay
with the night, without illusions,
on the wave
that seeks no shores,
in the boat of the shadow that carries it off,
not knowing
where it will land.

AND YET

And yet, throw nothing away.
Everywhere are hidden signs,
look behind the rotting fence, the wooden wall,
the old picture, into the empty jug,
behind solitude's door, inside the ruined house,
beneath a heap of ashes, beneath the fire's corpse,
beneath a calloused hand, beneath the roots of words,
beneath a stone, into a wound, into the face of fear,
at wasted pastures, behind a solitary bush,
somewhere a shelter is hidden, as yet unknown,
a gentle womb of poems and feathers,
of azure moss and breath
which may give rise
to an unheard-of harmony.

QUATTROCENTO

On the hilltops
amid this picture
I reencountered
that ineffable day
of childhood.

I entered

into that space
created for me,
into those valleys,
where everything whispers
my words.

I advance
toward a city
of forgotten tales,
toward emerald green
mountains,
as though I have found
my homeland.

BLACK REGIONS

A region where the air
still smells
of burnt sacrifices.
I hang
funeral wreathes
above it
on every cloud.

A region where
weapons of death
have ravaged meadows
hugging stone.
Above it I unfurl
a fabric of verse,
weave memory
and the smoldering dark
together.

A region where betrayal
has forged its knives.
I sprinkle it with dew,
cover it with ashes,
and bound,
pitch headlong in.

THE LIFE OF A CAPTIVE

I have been held captive
beneath an arch of frigid shadows,
and yet not a day has passed
but that I've seized morning by the shoulder
and walked through locked doors
toward the forbidden light.

This is how I know: there are moments
when everything is open — the earth and stars,
signs in the heavens, spiral mists.
The path of worlds,
shining spheres are close by
as I pass through the great equinox
into regions where the morning star
holds temporal sway.

From hope's charred remains
I keep fleeing to the northern cold,
the dark-blue chill, the slate-green ice,
and desires flicker in me
like the northern lights.

Then I return to the familiar ridges,
youthful memories flowing
like blue streams between them,
go out amid strange winds
bearing scents
from a southern sea.

Storms set to, fall hoarse,
I awake then on coral islands,
gaze at flocks of flying fish
as the soul hovers
over waves, amid reflections
like a white seagull.

I know of ivory coasts,
of palms over sheltering inlets
where nymphs with dazzling eyes

beckon in the water.
I know of wilds where
my thoughts race like gazelles.
I step through ruins
where the old gods
whisper their names.

The tropic of anxious days
keep binding me
to a gutted tree.
I break loose and escape to a land
of springs and unknown flowers
where I seek the orchid of wonderment
and where a playful gust
writes in the grass
the words that I whisper —
My heart is made of light and desire,
I cannot remain a captive.

THE SHEPHERD

Day was a
lime tree in blossom.

The breeze lies in the grass,
drunk with
nectarous dew.

A horse grazes
in the sky.

A shepherd, cloaked
in a fur made of clouds,
chases it home.

A child
stretches out in the moss.

A bush covers him
with the fragrance of berries.

His hands form a slumbering nest
for bumble-bees returning
toward evening.

THE SMELL OF MOWN GRASS

As I watch you, earth,
in evening's billowing light,
I tremble to your summons,
and the bitter taste of parting
floods my mouth day after day.

I am your eye, your heart,
your soul, your memory,
your rainbows fan out in me,
the eyes of countless hearts gaze out from me,
and the faithful mouths
of past love speak.
There shines in me the scent
of unknown women,
in me your years
respire.

I carry the hushing of forests
vanished long ago,
the smell of mown grass
uniting
birth and death.

Like a dark, secret spell
I speak these words,
and as I walk through short grass
in the sorrowful wind and mellow light,
this fragile creature can sense
that it's you that speaks them,
you speak them.

GREGOR STRNISA

THERE WAS A TIGER HERE

I.

A bright spring rain fell the day through.
The branches drip, the sand in the lanes is damp yet.
The sky has cleared. Slowly you go through the park,
the sun of evening haunts it, apparitionlike.

In the illumined peak of the dark tree,
a blackbird sings and sings. The evening's very quiet.
The sunlight turns wine red. And on the lawn,
there shimmers a bronze monument.

Just then you spot in the wet ground before you,
the wide, the clear, the deep impressions.
The park is very big, sunstriped, and full of shadows.
You start, go on, but know: a tiger came this way.

II.

You still remember well the day
when first you saw the tiger's trail.
You had just woken, and there it was.
Morning was like evening, full of shadows.

That was oh so long ago.
The night of that morning, you lay alert in the dark,
then fell into mazy sleep, like gazing out a window
and beyond it softly snows and will not stop.

You live as if not much has changed, really.
Soon after that morning, autumn came,
then we had the long, the damp winter,
and wet snow covered a dark city.

III.

You sit, elbows on the table, you look out the window.
It is late afternoon, soon to be dusk.
Not a sound will come into the room now.
You think how, outside, the winter day is fading.

You see just a piece of the sky and a roof, it is red,
likely the snow slid from it in the noontime sun.
In the last of light, the chimney casts a feeble shadow.
Evening will be leadblue, you think, and a little foggy.

You go to the window. A woman in white walks in the street,
across the way a child plays in the sand,
a summer day flickers in the darkened trees.
Like a great shimmering cloud, fades the summer day.

IV.

Maybe not much has changed, at all.
It's just that in rooms where once you were already,
you fail to find a favorite picture on a wall,
now there's only a pale rectangle there.

More and more often on your familiar routes,
tall, dusty horsemen cross your path.
Places you walk in, day after day,
bronze heavy monuments suddenly occupy.

And sometimes, entering a familiar house,
you find yourself in a cellar, stale and squat.
It was not there before. And huge snarling dogs
are tearing at their chains outside in the gardens.

V.

So you live, you're always off to distant places,
down foggy seas, up snowy mountain ranges,
you see so many new, so many foreign cities,
in whose small quiet squares you love to sit.

There, too, on the smooth pavement, from time to time,
dark, broad stripes stand out in the slanting sun.
You pick up a stone, you weigh it in your palm,
you murmur absently: There was a tiger here.

But him, himself, you haven't met yet.
Whoever the tiger looks at soon dies.
Always he pads before you, through summer's dark door,
through the white, fog chambers beneath December's skies.

SNOW

They're not eternal, these heavens,
these absent galaxies,
not eternal, this blue star forlorn —
only we mourn.

We mourn as a small creature,
in the hills, sometimes, mourns away,
except that maybe our hurt is deeper:
will the memory stay?

Will the two of you ever, in memory, here,
as you did, live again — will the memory go?
Will you be, at least, without the memory, together?
Will she, will you know.

THE INFERNO:
Part II. The Mountain

1.

Its two peaks are never obscured by mists.
The highest crags are clearly visible.
No one can say why, but still it seeems
that mists perpetually enfold the mountain.

The sky is blue, without the slightest cloud.
The sand is yellow. It glows dully in the sun.
The desert all around is flat to the horizons.
The mountain, like the smell of dirt, is black.

It juts up from the plain like the fist of a giant
that lies mostly buried deep in sand,
at dusk it's like the head of a bull's carcass,
its forehead broad and flat, with hollow eyes.

3.

The wind is chained to the mountain like a wolf,
while silence wails in its depths.
Whoever enters it goes groping blindly
through the long, low trenches of the labyrinth.

Many wander into dead-end passageways.
Trapped in the narrows, they die of thirst and hunger.
Each of them starts raving in his death throes,
imagining he's living as he did before:

inviting friends to banquets, or picking
cool spheres of fruit from dewy trees.
The last echo of his own delirious laughter
falls like a white mask onto his lifeless face.

5.

In the mountain's depths, in its far-off heart,
in the final, narrowest chamber of the labyrinth,

the Minotaur stands waiting in the lofty dark.
Delirium's creature: human, with a bull's dark head.

Whatever happens here takes place in silence —
an encounter in a land of endless night,
a sudden recollection of a distant morning, snowy white,
an eye that glimpses you, but which you don't notice.

Only very few attain these regions.
And none of them has come back from the mountain.
Some perish in the maze from thirst and hunger,
the Minotaur impales the others on its horns.

DANE ZAJC

THE BIG BLACK BULL

The big black bull roars into the morning.
Big black bull, who are you calling?
The pastures are empty.
The mountains are empty.
The ravines are empty.
Empty as the echo of your call.

The big black bull roars into the morning.
As if heavy black blood was spurting
to the tops of the dark pine trees.
As if over the wood to the east
was opening to the morning
a bull's bloody eye.
Big black bull, who are you calling?
Does it give you a thrill
to listen to the echo
return your hollow call?

Big black bull, the morning is bloodless.
You voice falls into the ravines
like a ragged flock
of black crows.
Nobody hears your loneliness.
Nobody drinks
the black blood of your voice.
Shut up, big black bull.

The big black bull roars into the morning.
The sun in the east sharpens
the gleaming slaughterer's axe.

THREE UNTITLED POEMS

Her body's ice melts
beneath his hands.
An autumn of fruit wakening beneath his fingers.
The autumn of her body.

Your body smells
like moss growing under fruit, he tells her.

And when he tells her,
two forests of stubborn thoughts
race to opposite side of the sky.

Their caressing hands demolish
the sheer rock faces between their eyes.
I'm drunk with your legs, he tells her.
I'm the mist in the rainbow of your breath,
she answers.
My body is christened with your scent,
she whispers.

Then they lie quite still.
And deep, deep below them is the moon
of two forests locked in ice.
But they lie quiet on the surface of silence.
So quiet that they can hear
a great, high dam grow up between them.
Cold water splashes down it.

***

Beyond the passes the eye of God molds,
keeping watch, protecting its tribe
differently.

Beyond the passes heads turn
lightning fast to fog.
Hands evaporate before they move.
Only gestures in the air still circle, silver.

Beyond the passes, friends and lovers,
acquaintances bid farewell fast.
Footsteps into the air.
Their gaits jingle.

Beyond the pases are no tracks.
No signs to make the paths.
No paths, most likely.
Beyond the passes, passes vanish.

Goal and purpose sink beyond the passes
into a nap with lead for brains.
Beyond the passes friends long since vanished
dance again. Oh yes, they dance.

High in the air they prepare us their dance
and occasionaly call out a word.
A fairly vanished and lonely word.
Their faces bent down, their faces suspended
not far from our eyes, they speak it.
A word with no meaning, crumbled off beyond the passes,
they stick it on our foreheads. Oh yes, they stick it there.

***

They built a cathedral of stone and their own thoughts.
Painstakingly they painted images onto the blue of its windows.
Carved monster which they carried in themselves
and wished to be rid of. Thoughts of themselves.
Those that they liked.
They built a city out of stone, mortar,
iron, glass, aluminum.
Bright, expansive, secure. To last forever.
They bordered the streets with trees and
amid the trees set out ponds with fountains.
But that wasn't till later. Not until
they started dying out.
Then they invented mirrors. They set them along the streets,
in rooms and meeting places.
They saw themselves arriving and departing in the mirrors.

They saw their actions in the mirrors.
They couldn't bear the sight.
And so they removed their equipment and machines
and hid in the mirrors.
Before that they set traps in the streets.
For the newcomer who didn't know their ways
and would pry about their abandoned habitats.

GOTHIC WINDOWS

At night the rubies commence to glow
on your breasts, Magdalena.
Two red rubies under a grey veil.
In the gloom of the cathedral.
In the white smoke of snuffed candles.
Throw off your veil.

Throw it off: the dry rustle of sin
in the odor of prayers.
With a dry smack the stars will fall
from your head.
In a bright stream the stars will pour
from your eyes into my open mouth.
The rubies of your body
will drop into my lap.
The moon will be licking your lips
with its red tongue of passion.

Throw off your veil, Magdalena.
Tomorrow you will stand in the spraying
light of the sun
naked. Humiliated.
Mine.

FOUR-LEAF CLOVER

Report of an injury (1):

A hole in the crown
of the head made by a blunt object.
The lilac bloom
of the brain shows
the uneven pulsing of thoughts.

A crossing

First he negotiates it in his dreams.
Rides over it on a white horse.
On a peacock.
On a striped heifer.
Or he chases the pig
that escaped —
he wakes up and thinks
he's on the other side.

He wakes up and thinks
he's on a different path:
patches spread from under his skin,
feathers shot out from his itching joints.

Then he wants the truth of his own crossing.
Dead soldiers wait in ambush there
aiming at him with dead arms.
The creator of all things set out tracks in the middle,
he ascertains.

He sneaks past the ambush,
must slip by in god's footsteps,
so he mutters spells.

Singing, a girl responds who has taken a paring knife
to her heart.
And the silence of corpses sucking onto the tails of neurons

like industrious fungi.
And the silence of god, cocooned in the yolk of nothingness.

When he stands still, his fingers try to stop
the stream of pain on his skull.
When he glances around, he is in
the very place he started.

Report of an injury (2):

The brain's blossom rapidly shrinks.
Pulsing of thoughts uneven.

Microscopic analysis:

A foreign object,
like an insect,
has pierced the cornea.
It penetrated quickly to the brain.
Suddenly the thoughts
ceased to beat.
They crumpled up,
shrank into death's cauliflower.

SNAKE KILLERS

If you meet an enemy
your snake should bite him.
But only those who like themselves
and have much confidence
do this.

Those who dislike themselves
look for solitude, to meet their snake in.
To exchange looks with it.
To endure its stare.
Soon after they're found dead
from a wound as slight as hunger's flower on blue lips.

Little is known of the mysterious power of the snakes's eyes,
because it kills only in solitude
and the traveler often mistakes it for dew glistening on a green leaf.
When someone cries out in the forest, we assume a hawk is killing a bird.

It's no crime if we kill someone with our snake,
or if we decide to go off to meet it.
Both are only forms of self-torment.
Much worse is when we kill someone else's snake —
he will crawl for the first heavy shadow
and at evening the sun's last remains will absorb him.

Nothing is known of the fate of snake killers.
It's unlikely they suffer or are punished.
They come from worlds that we can't know.
We don't know if they're the ones who leave at the stroke of the moment
that just passed.
We don't know if they're the ones who give us orders from behind our
fingernails,
or if they are the ones who step out of the dark wall of the future.

We never know which snake killer
hunts us through the rock quarries of the world.
And though we never know where our snakes are,
they always come at our call and perform our deeds.

Each one has his own snake and star.
But stars' unseen beams only rarely pierce
a leaf in the underbrush of our moments.

SOWER-HEAD

On the nonroad along which the steps pitter-pattered
the pain on the head's western continent said:
I've been building this hive for ages
and filling it with honey which you don't taste,
which is alien to you,
which you won't drink because I am filtering it
out of your flesh.

In the place called now, later, or always, the steps come
to a halt,
because the foot said:
I am sick of my name.
It will be no use rolling it round your tongue anymore.

Nobody saw the head that rolled down the slope
with a mask of earth and stuck with band-aids of
decay:
I am coming back forever. I am coming back to
freedom, it sang,
drunkenly scattering teeth
and happily losing eyes in the wet grass.
It rolled to a halt in a ravine
and crouched and took a long time wasting to
perfection.

From here it is impossible to see anywhere.
Nowhere do we find the one who was robbed,
who scattered.
To think of him is harder
than to think of the hole after the tooth is gone.

THE GARDEN

He came back shriveled.
Only the furrow behind him in the yellow sand
showed that he was moving.

From their perches the lookouts reported:
something is coming out of the desert.
They gathered on the border.
They pulled him into the world of green.
I am the one you sent, he said.
It was like pincers talking
when he spoke.

Then his head slumped down,
impaled on a willow wand.
He's not one of us, they thought,

and gazed at this doggish tongue
licking the grass.

What news from the Forbidden, they asked.
It's all true, he shivered,
and the pincers of his mouth closed shut.

They dropped water onto his tongue and demanded:
Isn't there a garden on the other side?
Isn't everything we don't have in that garden?
Everything you know is true, he rustled.

This isn't the one we sent, they said,
and slit his vein.
Then the slow grey liquid came oozing out of it,
they were sure
he was a hostile being.
They left him there. (His ribs thinned to
sticks of brushwood.)
They chose a new messenger.

THE KING

Made of old disintegrating chains,
of riddled iron,
with a handsome face
eaten away by the kisses of discarded women,
a stranger to himself and me,
— a king stood before me,
crowned with a crown of dark thoughts.

Where are your kingdoms, king, I asked him.
He nodded his head towards the evening side.

I looked at his hand.
A hand that had killed. All it held dear.
With iron fingers. Wormy with rust.
With five rings. All of them blinded,
for the ravening birds of the morning had stolen their jewelled eyes.

Where are your corpses, king, I asked him.
He nodded his head towards the evening side.

And I remembered a king with gold in his eyes.
With a golden mouth, with a golden smile between soft teeth.
With a heart of white moonlight.
A king I had known. I had wanted.

Where are you, king of my nights, I asked him.
He nodded his head towards the evening side.

And the king stood before me.
A king with a rusted face.
A king with beetles in his breast. Ravening beetles.
With gaudy eyes. Made up of the colors of sorrow and evil.
Wanting me with a gesture of his iron hands. For Himself. Himself alone.
As a king's slave.

What do you want from me, king, I asked him.
He nodded his head towards the evening side.

And when I looked towards the evening side,
I saw shadows over a river of plague.
And golden corpses dancing in the shadows.
With shattered jewels in their breasts.
And in the river, defeated life
floating towards the hungry mouth of the evening land,
and the king, who fired in my breast
the dark image of a king's hatred.

FAITH

Your heart comes to rest
deep under the ruins of your broken body.

And you think you are laughing.
But that is a sob running through your perforated throat.
And you think you are sobbing.
But laughter's sadistic fingers
stretch the skin of your cheeks.

68

Laughter rolls pebbles
around your mouth.
Then you toss into the air the colored beads
of your words.
Catch them with your mouth
and swallow them voluptuously.

For you can never fall.
Not to the bottom.

Then comes a stray dog
and laps the rainwater
from your open skull.
Lively mice gnaw
your ears.
Your lips.
Rats weave a nest
in your breast.

Then you laugh gaily
with your naked teeth.

You get up white pure and insensible.
You stand on the threshold of a new day.
The sun puts a bugle to your lips.
A hot brass bugle.

You have never fallen.

FOOTPRINTS

He'd come out to the edge of the forest.
He'd stop there, resembling
the swaying shadow of a branch,
while his face was like snow
frozen to the grass. As though he were fiercely
looking down from heaven, quickly
melting all the while.
He wasn't the kind easily
approached;

not filled with many words.

Once he broke silence. He spoke ponderously,
with words that echoed in evening's
church like a gob of curses.
Then he receded behind tree trunks,
scornfully melting among them,
and when they came to look for him, they confused him
with shadows, of which there were many,
easily grasped.
They played this game till
night cut short their footsteps.

Next morning strangers
brought a bier.
He lay on it —
two patches of hair, matted and rumpled
in a struggle with one
so complete that it left
no footprints.
Even the bier contained nothing, except for
that hair,
and even this the wet snow covered quite soon.

LUMP OF ASHES

For a long time you carry fire in your mouth.
For a long time you hide it.
Behind a bony fence of teeth.
Squeezing it within the magic circle of your lips.

You know that no one must sniff
the smoke from your mouth.
You remember that crows kill the white crow.
Therefore you lock up your mouth.
And hide the key.

But one day you feel the word in your mouth.
It fills the cave of your head with echoes.

Then you start to look for the key to your mouth.
For a long time you look.
When you find it you unlock the lichen of your lips.
You unlock the rust of your teeth.
Then you look for a tongue.
But there is no tongue.
Then you want to utter the word.
But your mouth is full of ash.
And instead of the word a lump of ash
stirs in the soot
of your throat.
Then you discard the rusty key.

You make yourself a new tongue of earth.
A tongue that speaks words of soil.

VENO TAUFER

OPEN-AIR CONCERT

she with tin legs
hourglass in mouth aquarium in her head
he with all the towns staircases on his back
under his arm a heart that can be wound up or
stopped

they open a book and look for a road
to water sky and blossoming grove
where there's no sweating paper no fumbling eyes
where like in a B picture pretty birds twitter

she opens her legs unlocks the aquarium
starts hunting for fish
he climbs the stairs and winds his heart up

nude bodies drown in sand from the hourglass
fish flick through their veins
with dark designs concealed in their bloody gills

HAMLET 69

each night is a slipping under the surface
listening to the rain as it rots the pile of papers
until in the cup of the morning eternity passes
the sun rises flicks out the razor

your face is wakened by a sliver of metal
you sense the feel of your vein beating
eye hears hand tongue touches time
you rejoice at the life of the razor

your image is mirrored in it
and the world neatly round it
closer to the world's center you spin

whole worlds on the narrow blade with you
suddenly potent to destroy
what destroying is destroyed

NON-METAPHYSICAL SEQUENCE

1. When I Touch You

brother who
where is
sister moon

only sand
brother who brother where only fire
only dust

and sister
dear body
death only brittle ashes

brother who neither hell
nor desert
when I touch you

death I become me
become you
I step into myself

death going into you
dusty stones hhrsskk
apes hhrsskk paper cups
brother air no breath gone
into father air into mother moon into her mother
into earth into everything into the whole thing into death

2. Is Burned by the Wick

pleading not cursing
from behind panes
from equator to icy leningrad

without a voice without the child of fire
it burns
through the wholeness into the bone

falls backward makes itself at home
yet stays awake
a hole in a dream

the wax of the translucent candle
is burned by the wick
it pleads

the sun into ashes
it revitalizes itself
into feathers of suns

stars only wind always farther
silence into its shine
writes and wipes

an old man with his stick in sand
happy sand
in sand

3. In the Air it Spreads

a king i am a king
in the air of air
in the air of the living dead
who are only doors
museum dogs doors of doors
and of the dead who will live

a living king of the dead
of the living dead the dead king of the living
the shadow which falls

upon the dust of a feather
which flies
through the doors of others

across the thresholds of others
to the door of its own breath
to the threshold of its own cry

upon the air
in the air it spreads
into the air

the king
ing
ing

4. *The Mud The Chill*

a slap of wind not a trick of memory
not death but a rent of emptiness
a smile of pale teeth

a center a space bitten out
a seam unravelling
the humility of the slayer of children

the pale namelessness of clearing
which leaves for all around
the mud the chill

desalination of tears
not a road
not an endlessness

but a plain but with no boundaries and
no limits not even a stench any more
only the slime a smudged cold

5. So How Long Will Time

silence sets into the darkness
the tide of calm rises
in mute thought

it kills without a groan
so how long will time
turn

how long will time
revolve
so how long will time

it is without us
how long will it run
without stopping

time
without end
without us

it remains
a long time
in the sun without the sun

it is killed at the end without end
an open space with no road
a wandering foot wading the silence

6. That One Can Even Hear the Clods of Earth

i rise up out of the liquid
of words i look for a shore
fog and creeping things

unreal cliffs not an echo
rising with no boundary or limit
spreading but without the stench

no weeds from the depths
i lift out my limbs
a wind never tiring

and what a dance
so unreally there
that one can even hear the clods of earth

which have been lifted by the very
silence of death can be heard
even as my body stiffens

i pull my fingers one by one
out of steam out of mist out of speech
nothing without the clay out of stillness

which rises among the glistening of feathers among prophet's
burning thorns
now there is no shore no island only murky waters
only the steep wave of ice

7. Perhaps the Juniper Needles

this pain is not to be survived
the luminous rain
which cries through the airless space

unless beyond the monotony of sound
through its fissures there is

78

that dust perhaps that pollen

which no spider web can catch
nor even the darkness of memory
just this no more after that come the words the voices

the wizard letters the runefrost
perhaps the juniper needles
perhaps the unsurvivably sweet motion of a blade of grass

moving to the white breath of the fleet dragon
before the maw that space vanishing along teeth into a darkness
blue beyond the azure of candles

now the drops the drops just this
what kind how long
how many drops

what are the limits
as the memory curves
in upon itself

8. *The Sloped Horse*

     saint george always
comes around
     the wind swift
everything slides askew
     the spear juts out
on the spear
     george the knight the dragon
the sloped horse
     the virgin beside him

9. In the World

       beyond the glitter
of the wind
       across the sea
i approach
       the horizon
the edge of the eye's pupil
       that image
which is turned
       and embodied
and thus returned
       from the black
light
       of the abyss

KAJETAN KOVIČ

ELDERBERRY HOURS

This is the old elderberry behind the house. These,
the elderberry hours.
The terrifyingly green tightness of the leaves.
The blackish tint of the berries.
The bitter elderberry time before the storm.
Below the wall, the blossoms of the nettle.
The grass unmown.
Behind the wall, a room.
The stale smell of bachelor uncles.
The hollow elderberry stalk of Sunday.
The after-dinner quiet.
The reddish stems of the berries.
Their flat, insipid taste
in elderberry sleep.
Sweet spittle ripens
in the sluggish mouth of boys
leaning on the elderberry flanks of houses.

THE WATER OF LIFE

comes and knocks
softly at first like rain in the early morning
on the windows of diners
where workmen drink their hurried teas
comes from the lukewarm air
from the glass autumn
tasting of the mountain in blossom
and the thrill wolves feel
and just touches hands and feet

and skin the whole body over
comes with the vertigo of windmills
screws
and strong machines
into the mad
dynamic day
into the white heart of the world
comes and says:
I am the water of life
where do I flow
where do I flow

FRUITS OF THE SUMMER

You went through the cold trees
you invisible you to-be,
whipped by the rain
and icy winter
crazy for this life
and not a hope in the world

you carried your sweet bodies
that had been thrown into other embraces
out of a dark foreign delusion
pure again over and over
over to our side of the world

frail and shy you went
through flowering
relentlessly herded
toward your perilous fate
unsure till the end

and then with a shout you smashed
the happy gate
and spilled over the earth

white white white
fruits of the summer

RAIN

Rain is making a racket in the gutter,
an insistent, wistful, tinny hum,
spread across the acacias,
across their intense, waiting scents.
The dogs stare vacantly at the yellow horizon.
They scent the hunt, and the wet, alien animal.
A mild evening is on its way.
The wall is sticky and sweating.
The boys stroke the wet dogs
and their own tight unknown bodies.

GARDEN OF GOLD

The chill and the damp under the pine tree.
The long shadow over the dark house.
Grapes, blue as dreams.
In curtained rooms,
dying fathers,
whose punishment is sons
left behind in wars,
entranced by the cuckoos' singing.
In the garden, the yellow autumn hour,
and under sweaters,
the warm breasts of girls,
as they lie down horizontal
under the curiosity of boys,
and as above them, blue as death,
ripens the isabella.

BOYS

The dawn is unstoppable.
In bodies, the cold and the glow and the shadow and everything.
The promise of the world.
The anguish of eternal light.
The wonder of white flowers.
Of the deadly mingling with the unknown.

And the terror of departure,
when, their backs bare,
before the wall in ruin,
they stare into the endless morning,
alone for good.

SCENTS

In the ordinary morning,
the stirring smell of dry grass,
the taste of dregs,
the wet scent from the cellar
and the earthen light
out of sudden dreams,
when there stand before the door
the white shapes of the dead
and sniff like docile dogs
the house and the doorstep
and the dark corridor
in which boys
of an early evening
first feel the quiver and terror of girls.

FEVER

The hills are piled up in the noontime.
The stableboys come driving
the wet mares up from the river.
In the bushes hang
the swollen cornel berries.
Pale red shadows
rustle under the oak trees.
A strange milk
drips from yellow flowers.
It's going to be cold.
There's some terror in the air.
Young boys bolt across the stubble field
and in the dark, solitary wood
tremble like little dogs.

THE TASTE OF SPRING

Water gathers
into patches of flowers
frosts singe
lips and heart
the wind shakes lovers
like the frailest bushes
pine needles fill
their veins
twilights over the river
are so thin and pale
evenings are hollow
like doghouses with the dogs gone
anguish squats
in every finger
in every fingernail
there is a miniature terror
so all at once
do the alders darken
their somber band
plays in the breast
and in the mouth there is
the senseless desire
for the sweet taste
of Saint John's wort.

SUN

The grass-to-be beneath the soil
sips warm, melting snow.
Brooks are in flood, springs aboil,
the pregnant rivers' bellies grow.

Through the pine forest thick,
full of witches, full of specters,
trailing black hounds in a pack,
goes the green squad of hunters.

Though all creatures be in flight,

though the snow-bound heart benighted
feels no mercy yet,

behind the woods, the sun grows,
and in the clearing, fear flows,
a drop, for now, into a hunter heart.

LABRADOR

White is the rivers' roar
in Labrador's dark taigas.
Far away the foggy shore.
With hills between. And seas.

There is the pine wood solitary.
There is the breath of place, perpetual.
There is the fragrant, resiny bark.
There is the ripe, red berry.

There are the green lights of the cypresses,
spread out to the dawn.
There are the fires of southern stars.
And hills and seas, and on and on.

LAND OF THE UNBORN

Land of the other side of the world.
Of shadows made. Of white air.
All alone and unfulfilled.
Which flames. Which waits there.

Which is nought. And all at once all.
Thrown into the impossible.
A tale which happens, yes. Or, no.
Which wants to happen. So!

Which past dark berries stares.
Pale and without ornament.
Which has unbelievably eyes

of a time not come yet.

Which is outside the door. The window. Here.
In the colt's foot. In the dandelion.
Far away beneath the frozen mountain.
Far away there, with the holy ghost.

A white bird, silent, flying
ceaselessly through zone on zone,
one wing made of what is coming,
one, of a longing for home.

SVETLANA MAKAROVIC

MIDSUMMER NIGHT

I.

Bewitched, the wind dies down.
The evening sun floods the forest.
Long, warm tunnels underground
house golden foxes.
They raise their snouts, eyes shining yellow.
Outside a cuckoo calls.
A dappled bug crawls out of bracken.
Green sparks flicker under moss.
New springs surge forth from underground
in places where they've never been.
The nymphs are approaching, nymphs are approaching.
Bristly beasts bound down forests paths.

II.

A swarthy smith uses the moon for his anvil.
The forest catches in its thousand echoes.
A white fire flares up in the glen.
It holds fast, shines, transparent and pure.
Ladylike, the foxes
fan themselves with ferns no longer ferns.
The cuckoo flaps its wings, becomes a screech owl,
the gray screech owl calls excitedly.
Faces are transformed in the space of a scream.
Only the dappled insects take cover.
I've followed you, my handsome deer,
you've fixed me with your great, gold gaze
and now step toward me.

III.

The sun bursts through the pine trees.
No tracks remain in the dewy grass.
It's quiet and very light.
In long, warm burrows underground
sleeping foxes breathe,
their tails athwart their eyes. Insects, possibly dead,
have fallen from the branches.
In the glen a flowering bush exudes scent.
Somewhere a cuckoo calls wearily.
No one answers.
Join me, it sings at once. Today will be pleasant,
a pleasant summer awaits us.

THE SNAKE

I.

Like a noble fire,
poison flares in it.
It winds through smoldering stones —
a slender, cold sovereign.
Stretching out in the sun's palm,
and staring in its face.
It kills every shadow
that falls across its pure body.
Aspiring to be a golden skeleton
when fall returns.

II.

It shuns returning to darkness.
It dreams of dancing
slow, sad dances;
its shadow is gold in the dark.
Poison blazes in it,
green and bright.
It wears no masks.
Each night holds up to it an awful mirror.

Each night wraps a black chain tight around its neck.
Each night it keeps watch, black, heavy in damp sand,
awaiting the distant sun.
Its flat grimace growing more and more bitter.

III.

It danced a grim dance of death
on a pile of stones.
The sun withdrew its hands.
September breathed through the grass.
It went taut as a spear and collapsed.
It had wanted to be a gold skeleton
when fall returned.
But when fall came it was
just a blasted branch in the bleary air.
The grater of summer would
never consume it to the end.

ANTHILL

I.

All the same. I am the same.
You are the same. All of us.
Our larders full. Never enough.
We need more. Don't like strangers.
That are different. No.
Or light in the kitchen. Eye on the door.
We have. To have. Will have.
The same. It's good. It's right. Don't think.

II.

This day I'm a whoop.
The wind airs my downy feathers.
I'll sing and fly, my death
will be a drop of forest air
for the bright wind to drink.
The great forest shines and shines.

At nightfall I expand into a huge predator,
and my sharp beak glows golden.

III.

In the big house there are people living.
They whelp plump children, satisfaction.
They stare at blind mirrors and nod.
Their eyes are neat, big buttons
that they fasten and undo.
They seize their things with hands.
They don't know about the golden beak —
opening above their roof.

THE BLACK MILLER

I.

I'm thirsty. Swamp river is bitter.
A willow's gaudy eye glares at me.
The fog stirs. Time now
for the swamp lights
that sting my eyes and scald my soles.
The water gulps my cry, I gulp the water.
They drowned me many years ago
for being faithless to my husband.

II.

The black miller draws a hex sign on his door
and goes to bed. No one can get in.
Inside is warm, fluttering darkness.
Till morning, malevolent footsteps in the mill.
All night I ride the millwheel outside
and weave a gown of wet moss.
I haven't been for quite some time. But since I used to be,
tell me, black miller, what's in your dreams?

III.

As morning sharpens above the drowsy
surface, a stinging whip lashes —
I flee. Over a water rat
so it squeals, through the willow so it shudders,
I escape into the reeds. I'm water,
a drop, a water bubble, steam —
and finally, the unwanted thought the black miller
brushes off as he steps out through his door.

NIKO GRAFENAUER

WIDOW

A widow is the silent shadow of a dead man
behind a faraway window. Outside night meshes.
Damp scenes materialize and fade upon the walls.
Like a ram, the wind butts the door.

She is alone among cloudy impulses. The wood in the room groans.
Her movements settle like pleats of air.
Twilight congeals in her softness.
Beneath her fingers a cigarette dies crackling like a louse.

THE SOLITUDE

Black solitude, cool forehead.
behind it gathered higher
than obliteration so alone, without memory
to drown in white.

farness, stretched to the light allures
towards finality.

flames of never appeased satiety
in an open coronal cup of shedding days,
though space is lasting, what enormity
of never ending fading in the air!

weight, dispersed to poppy seeds of moments,
is cumulating in the bodily tight
embrace of years, weight,
plasmatically spilled into the day, now
and here. over the bream that holds what is,

to the brink. is being
a bottomless abyss, measured
with a plumb of pain?

a wound gazing to a wound, an eye to an eye.
what wakefulness opening the eyelids!
is my blood blending with your pulse
within one circulation?

a farewell, felt by feelers stretched out
towards the lost. and within the soul, twice erased
height of the call with no fulfilment. under the dark
skies of the past in a halo, encircled
by Psyche longer than the light of a candle.
the murmur, gathered with intent to withold what
the silk reals, gently folded in distancing.

when will
the black-rimmed dawn appear, or a skylark, along with
a nightingale's song? two lumps of gravity in expecting bosom,
yet the voice with plagal wings is to the skies returned.

in gaping air, the riddle mutely hangs: its shadow facing daylight,
but towards the night it is hopingly spread
over the unanimous fall of two lives
into romeojuliet's embrace.
is there still anywhere more absence held in hands
so tightly joined?
on the lips a whisper drawn in a rime of semivowels,
translucent of imperfection, but for the living
a requiem, preserved for eavesdropping never ended.
in it, between the wrinkles,
hidden from the sight, lastingly shines a sorrowful tear
(carbon crystal's clearest water),
stuck with valences into soft stygian velvet.

an eye, reaching out of life to eternity,
with the look of the light years —
you but to perfection with the word:
Elisheba.

the time behind the eyelid stored:
immer und nimmer.
by fortuitous flesh grown into now:
ichundich, filled up to the throat
with the tears of eros.
added to death: a deafmute verse,
tasted on the lips.

pressed into the being's pressure what is and is not,
high, without egress. ever-
lasting weight, lulled towards the earth.
are the dreams from underneath another azimuth assembling?

neither a trap nor an exile, endlessly
within secluded circles.
a solution, trodden by the steps that follow
the nascent death in water, softly shaded
Neben-
leben.

between to come and to go, equationally interspaced
I-and-I.
how much in between collected into days!
where am I? the truth is even barer than bare,
and the nought is perfect: beyond the words
that keep my voice within themselves.

TIREDNESS

Winds bloat on the branches like a long restrained urge.
Silently you sink into the shadow-streaked forest
where winter petrifies the birds tearing themselves to pieces
for their bleary significance, your spirit circles like a baby monkey.

It is growing dark, the gallows stand like an empty door in your mind,
its shadow falls in your way. Tiredness looms behind your back;
if you glance across your shoulder, evil phantoms arise;
the waste country before you greens with spreading mould.

I AM

Noon at mid-summer is cruel as clear consciousness.
Whatever escapes numbness only in form is cut for prey,
Snakes twirl upward like wisps of smoke.
It is growning dark, autumn is distant and is drawing near.

With the laws of the dead I established freedom
in order to subdue it and ascertain everything.
Winds girdle me, it's a long climb.
The pain that I am enters into me like a knife.

Behind me full of evil composure lurks silence.
The fall is long like an outcry that dies in the distance.
Lost in silence I seek strength for a new venture,
but everything seems to rot in the grip of darkness.

THE HOUSE

The house where you think things over
is growing tense like a darkening day.
Memories close in
as if you were dying with gloomy dignity.

Silence shines upon the immobility
you take from the dead.
Loneliness gnaws you like verdigris.

In the narrow crack of permitted consciousness
projecting itself like a beam into dusk,
moths quiver.
Love throws your enlarged shadow against the wall.
With a clammy key I step towards the threshold.
I call from the verge of black forebodings
into emptiness.
Silence is your language.
     I grow quiet,
but within me, as in late autumn,
sounds flutter, almost tears.

The house where you think things over
is like the beginning of all that goes away.

HATE

Hate grows
like the shadow of a mountain towards evening.
In an invisible blaze it twists things.
Madness licks consciousness like smoke.

In twilight clairvoyants are crowned
with the efforts of their whole life.
Chained between silence and fasting
they read the world like the palms of their hands.

It is terrible, when I consider it,
to depart during sleep
without any weight,
without resistance like beauty,
when I consider it,

after all,
in spite of the dead,
man has experienced nothing.

HORROR

Sounds sleep in the black spangle of tightening waters.
Now and then they flap up a noise
like a man awakening from sleep.
Shadows blend with misunderstanding.

You lean over your thoughts as over a bleeding vein.
Your hair sprouts in the wind like grass
when you rub your hands and pant into the ovary
of horror flaming up in the middle of the night.

You are alone and time surrounds you like the circles of a tree.
Like a deep echo the world confronts you.

You go and your evening image
goes slowly dark, a sinking into forgetfulness.

Silence shatters at our touch.
Dust beneath your toes unclenches its numberless fists.
Rage licks the bristling adder
threatening you like god's finger in your home.

DROUGHT

The country where I walk rots under the feet of strangers.
Sharp winds seize the bristling grass.
Claws grab me from behind, I walk in a trap.
The landscape is like a blanket drawn over the dead.

Summer pours black thunder on the heavy seals.
Dryness floods my mouth and slowly chokes me.
The sickle pauses high in my consciousness.
I halt in flight, cast in a flash of lightning.

Time opens like the teeth of a wolf
bitten into the quivering world with the rapacity of cold.
Thirst swells slowly in my mouth like a poisoned fruit.
At the table when memories dusk over I read ruin
           from the palm of my hand.

THE WALK

        Slowly,
as if veiled
by a dying urge,
I walk among sombre winds
that bar my way.
Sometimes fatigue illumines me
like a dark flame.

Tree-roots
clench a handful of earth.
Owls shudder in their sleep

like heavy hours
and their wailing cries
flail into the night.

Summer
is a vigorous stir of light.
Phantoms bloom in a long beam.

THE SPEECH OF SILENCE

Stubborn forms still subdue you
and all that is ancient
in you, I mean these dark forces
full of passionate spittle
and feverish night sweat
that burn in gusts of confusion
like a shudder;
and then you are so unencumbered
when you walk without peace through the dark city
flattened by the falling snow,
you can sing within
like a hard crust of bread
in a bony fist.
Sometimes a black slit yawns
on the wall and through it
come the smell of mould, winter fruit,
urine and homeliness
and slowly disperses
in the bristling cold.

They accompany you
into the deaf underworld of earth
with the words you drank from
all your life
and now too
when the moist eyelid rises slowly
and beneath it the hunger of the earth
gapes at you,
no man has spoken of it yet,
because with it only shadows talk,

yet that moment of parting rings out louder
than all the rest —
the speech of silence.

TO EDVARD KOCBEK ON HIS 70TH BIRTHDAY

I have avoided you, great poet
and thinker, because you were too heavy
a burden. Fiercely I drew a line behind me,
in order to be at ease, light,

agile. An infinitesimal mote of sunlight,
dancing as it crunches the muses' host
for a joke and spits the seeds of all oranges
high in the air. You were

clearly powerful, not an orange. So that
they glint, so they show, so that children
point up at the colorful flying kites. I was
the apple tree unaware who had

watered its soil. Today I know who,
more than any among us, is the shaper
of our freedom. Now I am shaken
with feeling and I'll quickly raise my glass

to your health. You see, precisely because it's
a holiday I must continue
with my crunching. I sense that
joy strengthens with every moment.

IMMURED ALIVE

Communists use the same chairs, the same
stairways. There's blood flowing under their skin,
too. When they eat, they swallow. They look with their eyes,
their houses are hooked up to the same electric

current. For many years I had a communist for
a best friend. And my own
children: frightening examples of half communists, half
people. They're scattered. With communists it's always

either/or, and because they didn't liquidate
me at their height, they've missed their chance. Still
they retain all power and control, the clocks,
the bells, they can still tell your child

in broad daylight to his face, "Join us,
be a communist." They have mouths like ants
and do not reject property. They've been riveted
to the Central Committee building with nails. Walled

up in the corridors of power they call
innermost. Even though there's greenery all around,
even though there are plenty of trees all around, in the city's
center. Communists are a precise blow to

the blood. Their dew is inhaled invisibly.
And they go to their graves in peace, to music,
forever. Sad and shaken, as though
this were the same sort of death as ours.

[1986]

CHRIST AT HERMES' DOOR

Your face is buried, ounces of ice looking out from the block.
Is that you? Do I need a model for God?
Sweet, sweet, both of us humble and sweet.
Gas gathers in our teeth.

So that we grow blue fangs.
Who is that rubbing sand along our lips?
You are a vase. My hands caress you.
Clay spinning on a wheel.

When I shape your mouth with my palm, it stays.
Explodes. Changes color. Summons red from gray.
Does the fire caress you? Would your nails reek if they burned?
I wrap you around my forehead. You skin is a belt.

I think you are formed, perhaps just a little hard.
You hold water.
Will it fizz in you?
Will flower petals float on the surface?

Will they veer away from the sides?
Rush towards them?
Cool off? Will you need me to smash you?
Will you still want to run down my hands like honey?

I will carry you around on my shoulder.
Agree to all roles that are rustling, sweet and light.
You're the cream with which I summon cliffs from the earth's bowels.

I pull them out.

When all else has melted, they don't melt.
When vanilla and the liquified wings of my wood
flow at the earth's core. We do not combust.
Our fangs are made for this unbearable heat.

We are exhausted.
Alloyed, united like elephant and oak.
O, ear wax of the she-elephant!
Have I shoved you in it?

TORTURING THE SLAVE

Slave, will your breath halt?
Will the Slavs destroy the geography of their cabbage?
In the throat of a she-deer lies a lacquer globe
that my mother had eaten.
On it a picture of Jerusalem, on it only.
Did you make the grass grow?
Tie threads on bombshells?
Make gold out of fireclay?
My blotting paper lies in a crystal moor
and it is your fault, slave!
Just look at my optical gargantua.
Knives, like the bubbling water of occult races,
are uniting with the gauze on my finger.
What are you waiting for?
Why don't you stop the weather just
like highlanders used to in olden times?
They cut down everything obstructing the wind,
snapped brambles and chopped them up.
Rolled oak trees down.
Timber-slides came later,
after gravitation had won.
You are crying, son, because of being soaked,
but your calendar is not in the spirit of the Maya.
Your hips seem to be stolen from
my mountains in Crete and when
barbarians will stamp on them with their boots
you'll leave the revolving door
so white-hot from the solitude
of the she-deer, that stags will dash into
the forest, already smelling of other burned
stags, and sing the last pious accord of their
suicide.

Nations that forget their story-telling
die out. Smelling of ointment they
have direct access to the heart of the world.
They don't bother to recreate circles
anymore, or run in
the snow, barefoot.
Nations that forget their story-telling
don't tremble anymore under the weight of incomprehensible
powers, the stars they used to gaze at
are themselves. They become
the stars —
the nations that live in grace and luxury.
When they wake up, there, on their left side
lies a handsome young
Arab. They make love to him day and
night, when he dances or
speaks. They pitch their omnipotent
tent over him, the nations that
forgot their story-telling.
The nations that forget their
story-telling are simply wiped out by
passion, all their elegant and meaningless
life is absorbed in the knife
of the horsemen, of the comrades, of the people, that sent
Hassan.

EPITAPH

Only God is. Ghosts are apparitions.
The blind shadows of machines that conceal the Kiss.
My Death is my Death. I do not share it
with the warm tranquillity of others, annulled under the sod.

You, who will kneel on my grave,
the earth will shake. I'll pull the sweet juice from
your nape and genitals. Give me thy mouth.
Watch out that a thorn doesn't pierce

your ear-drum as you roll like a worm
alive in front of the dead one. Let this
bomb of oxygen wash you gently, gently. Blow up only

as much as your heart can bear. Get up and
remember: I love all who have insight into me.
For ever. Get up now. You surrendered and awoke.

SEED

I know a wrinkle is theophany
and my fingers
deer, starved to death.
When will a blossom die?
When will I be swept from the river banks?
When will the pulsing of my veins
become the apparition in a cup?
I know I am a memory of the sky,
dust, into which a poem
kneels.

FEBRUARY

There is a time when
pure emotions
invade us like
bags from the black pressed
leather
of a shark —
February. The month
of raked leaves under
the thick blanket of snow,
of pink snails, shut
in dark waters.
The light beams forcefully through
a fork and a knife.
Sandals and streets
on Crete
invade
the dining room

with a glow and dust.
It is time for drying fish up North.
In Denmark men in clogs
wrapped in wool
carry food into stony
halls. City buses
resemble
quiet polite
people.

ABOUT THE GOVERNING FORCES

I am a rock.
The bottom of pain the moon shines on, the sun not.
I am a train, unhitched,
that people don't greet from fences anymore.
I am the hay they burned
to awaken hunger in you.
I am smoke.
The broken circle of smoke, bluer than
plankton, that though it glimmers still eats the color of the sea.
My bosom is crushed.
Horses walled in.
A river that unglues itself from water
dries out the riverbed it used to run on.
A seed that grows up is dead magic aboveground.
Since where there is the trunk of an oak tree
there cannot be gentle
mists and swinging maple leaves.
The carpet in a parlor is red.
The noble color of parquet floor
is brutally covered by the products of the human hand.
In it there is the blood of slaughtered sheep,
that is why we walk so softly on it
until we are suffocated by the breathing of their
lives.

STAG

The deepest of rocks, the white white desire.
Water, that springs from blood.
Let my form shrink, let my body be crushed,
so it will all be in one: the cinder, the skeletons, the handful.

You are drinking me as you were pulling out the color of my soul.
Lapping me, the gnat in a tiny boat.
My head is blurred, I feel how
mountains were created, how stars were born.

You moved your temple away. I stand there.
Look, in the air. In you, who are merged with me now,
mine. The golden roofs are curving under us,

the pagoda's leaves. I am gentle and tenacious in
this huge silken sweetness. Pushing fog into your
breath, your breath into the divine head in my garden, stag.

WHITE ITHACA

stars, salute me
to spur the fire, the nape of a beast,
to spur the chill, arcadia
the flame of grapes in shade, the sound of a helmet

to open the sea to me, baptism, greed
the roaming of white sheep, burnt meat
so I can once again see the color, how it sails,
hear the chiming of our lady, of fallen balustrades

so I can give animals escape, bread to people,
sin to the gentle wind, a razor to wine,
so I can see the bauxite ships, the sun in the earth
chains on the walls, the tribe of days

you have to unite, stars, to burn out in blue
so no smell or crumbs will be left behind, no pictures or silence,
so I can yet see bamboo, native fields,
the quiet chewing of deer, the white ithaca

110

UNTITLED

On the border between Pennsylvania and Ohio
the sky is higher, the earth more leveled,
the slain wheat returns miraculously
as moss and snow, as silence.

Nature, the word melting in the mouth
like honey, long chained down in darkness,
is thawing at the roots. Distrustful fields,
mute flats, still offer a reflection,

shelter their body with a dead color, not to
be hurt by the quick, indifferent glances of observers.
The young, vulnerable tissue is generous only

to friends, piously suitable to the new
balance of creation, gracefulness of love,
shiny kisses soft as breath.

MILAN DEKLEVA

ANAXIMADER'S PROOF OF EXISTENCE

The sun has the diameter of my hunger:
at sunrise the size of my palm, and at sunset
the volume of breasts in ecstasy.
What a clear proof of greatness and existence!

ANAXIMANDER ABOUT CAUSES AND CONSEQUENCES

Is a nest knit to a circle because of the mobility of spheres?
Are the spheres mobile because of the nest being bent?
Am I human because of the language, or is the language human
because of me?

ANAXIMANDER'S POSTULATE OF PERFECTION

Things are falling to the opposite side
of their growth: the postulate of verticals.
Motion belongs to infinity,
immobility belongs to time: the postuate of horizontals.
Thought has its source in memory: the postulate of circulation.
Man rises into his future,
steps into his present,
and lies down into his past: the postulate of crossways.
Rejuvenation of the world is in its growing old:
the postulate of perfection.

ANAXIMANDER ABOUT THE HARMONY OF THE WORLD

The harmony of the world is based on the paradox of man.
The harmony of man is based on the paradox of the world.
Man is not the world: what a paradox!
Man is the world: what a harmony!

ANAXIMANDER'S POSTULATE OF THE DIFFERENCE

Between the life of traces and the traces of life
there can be no equation.

ANAXIMANDER ABOUT THE GENESIS OF MAN

When a man is born, he starts asking himself about things
which are older than he is.

ANAXIMANDER'S CAPABILITY OF EXCLUSION

I can imagine a print without a foot.
But I cannot imagine a foot without a print.
I can imagine a world without life.
But I cannot imagine life without a world.
What a horror!

ANAXIMANDER IS DREAMING

A rooster, spy of the light, has taken my head away
and bequeathed it to the river.
A bumble-bee, the stepson of the sun, has stung my shoulder
changing it into dew.
A raven, the charcoal purpose of the fire, has untied my navel
spilling me into the trembling sky.

I was awake.
A trembling body mourned without a shadow.
In the meantime the river has met the sky in the dew.

ANAXIMANDER'S COUNT-DOWN

Five senses for a single heart.
Four directions of the sky for a single earth.
Three dimensions for a single space.
Two creatures for a single child.
A single life for a single death.
No word for the infinity which links
the heart, the earth, space, the child, and death.

ANAXIMADER'S POSTULATE OF PARALLEL

I, Anaximander, a wedge driven into a woman,
half god, half puppy. My ionic penis
is strained in the iambic rhythm. We rub each other
to honor Love: the meaning of parallels is infinity. The meaning
of infinity is nothing. Without you I couldn't
be anything, I, Anaximander.

ANAXIMANDER'S WAKE

A silent house. A mouse-silent woman
is breathing her dreams beside me. Earth-silent
is my wake, scared, stunned, without a memory.
I wake, solemnly waiting, and touching my love
hot between her legs. What is it I am waiting for?
Nothing. Nobody. What is the purpose of such a horrible eternity?
Death? Maybe I no longer exist. An illusion.
Spirit is cruel, it wreaks vengeance upon the body.
It knows it will never grow old
as the body will. Time doesn't care.
Time destroys the silence of the house,
my wife's dream, and my wake.

ANAXIMANDER IS MEASURING

Staring to the stars, as gods used to.
A Greek by profession, charmed by relations,
seven times higher than my own feet,
seven times more silent than my own mouth which has spat out
the tongue found by the Forgotten One
in a small shrub. Staring to the stars.
A Greek by profession. I am realizing that the earth
floats, but not on water, as Thales believed.
I am not naive. I still transplant words
from the earth to the woman's joint, gardening solitude
of the dead: deeper from evil or goodness is
the blue indifference of beauty.

THAT WHERE WE LOOK AT

To look out
from the most tender touch of the two
who follow each other in lobe
like two same-sounding words in a dictionary.

Out, past, and beyond the will
or unsatisfaction,
or excitement
which separates things and their
perspectives.

Out, to a perfect plain and clear.
For a bloom is not to be understood
through the beginning of the bud,
nor through the fruit.
Neither is the essence
of silence.

As man is born from a farness
and for a distance,
so is all of importance already here.

To look out does not mean to look

into the strangeness of space,
for a body is borderless crumbliness
the soul only belongs to it
as much as
height belongs to a mountain.

That what we look to is time,
peculiarity of a stone,
a tormenting erosion of consciousness,
after
when outside itself
it recognized itself.

As man is born from here
and for here,
so is all of importance a distance.

That where we go is time,
        the attitude of unity.

HOMES OF VISION

In you I will mature,
spun between your thighs.

Deaf for duration.
Received by the silence of blood
I'll become a pulsating
inventory of destiny.

With eyes that drink
neither darkness, nor light, nor misproportion of shades,
with eyes flashing
ionized wonders of foreshapes
into the small tube of the umbilical cord,
I will be yours.
Yours forever.
Hidden from all that is not
the essence of flower,
of shell,

of music,
of passing away,
yet which — from moment to moment —
still touches them all.

You live the memory, giving to the supersensuous
images of sense.
In the ear, let's say, in the obelisk of autumn
you are building the hoarse
metropolis
of my unreality.
How many homes! For just a single illusion!

BLIND SPOT OF TIME

Sleep, my child.
Breathe innocence into the silence of the night.

Your face from inside shines.
Not in one, but in hundreds of layers,
in the mythical, simultaneous parallelism
of plans.
How many possibilities that aren't mine!
What a will to reach over all
who had gone
and now — as guardians — keep vigil in death:

Of whom?   Of what?

Blind spot of time,
all the love that was
reused
by the only woman and the only man
has poured into you.

Blind spot of time,
you are the only clearness
of space,
the only path wrung out of oblivion,
to be its only
little bride.

Blind little bride of time.

PLEASING ARE THESE REVERIES

What was concealed
behind the cross-examination of the being,
humped into writing?

Going through the sonnets of desires
reveals the solemn moments
of special happiness.

Pleasing are these reveries
of the skin in touch, these starry order-forms
of private eternity.
The souls are out of breath — down to the feet
out of breath — in the rooms which do not pass
the sublime death.

That which is outside, that which wordly
sanctifies, that is too hard to be
adapted to a shape.

But it holds: in the word,
in the smashed gum, in the judgement
that contradicts others but not itself.

Emptiness, the trap of love, you
subhuman destiny of writing poetry:

pathology of expression.

IVO SVETINA

ALMAGEST 44

Fidelity — what is your honeyed core:
whence do you come, clothed in pain,
and settle, like a bee, on your own harvest?

I hide from your severity,
find refuge with a sacrificial lamb,
to become one in an alien sin
which will be our ruin.

But — you are insatiable and it is not enough
that I have become a nest of pain,
a metaphor of love, who knows not who to love,
not to lose your fragrance, name,
the laws feeding on
fidelity itself.

A word or two, and you lie with me,
relentless to the flesh, which can no longer be
merely a name for something else.

ALMAGEST 60

I have no presentiments left, no hope —
intoxicated by the purity of the child
leading me through fire. Fatigued —
a sample of rock which has known
a million years, six frosty winters and a
summer of flood — I would sit with a bumble-bee —

in a meadow, at the edge of a young beech grove,

121

in a blooming poppy field,
and I would ask for a single inch of wisdom:
only to fly, to fly until
desire runs out and being gently
bids farewell — even to the bumble-bee:

to my anticipations, to my hope.
"Your heart is too heavy," hums the bee,
"forged at the bottom of your soul."

ALMAGEST 66

When I can no longer tell good
from bad, gold from honesty and
beauty from people — I will enter the house
built in the century of the sun,
and I will sell my eyes multiplied times without number
to the windows in its sun-flowery walls.

On the crown of my head grapes will ripen
from which they will press,
when they come armed with an answer to every question —
a single answer! — wine
to celebrate — pugnacious omniscent ones —
the birth of a new moral principle:

blood and tooth are sister and brother —
so do not ask me to kill this beautiful
kinship. You had better drown your heart
for decades to bear witness to the sudden
flood which has united all the living beings
in the Brotherhood of the drowned.

ALMAGEST 70

I go to the forest, and a sparrow through it, and before
a tree the name and the kind of which I do not
know for sure — but it is the sparrow's home —
we meet — two songsters.

The sparrow who has not yet experienced the burning of the wood
does not know I would like to be the song of his
singing life which in itself is
a tune — but to me a revelation, revealed in
an old wise man:

he did not sink into nothingness, he whom people
perceive as the one — the singing. I was crazed,
standing in the shadow of his home,
wider and more harmonious than any
of my songs and foreign wisdom.

ALMAGEST 78

I have never researched my own self!
I have never seen any of this,
heard nothing, leave alone read.
I have not been anywhere, lived . . . I don my
yellow frock and step to the water —
under pomegranates, lights in the
mysterious December blue,
they go off in the night and become
the capital and the table
for a flock of timid thievish starlings.

With their discordant chirping they build
the paper Chinese wall, no higher,
wider, deeper than the midday shadow.

I am of the one and only — countless —
Work —, which I have named gentle tranquility,
happiness, harmonious within, though artificial.
For I did not take it, or return to Nature, or
say what happened in the night
between 14. and 15. August, when, asleep, I saw her
adorned with a blemish — dawn, pink
sweat of the water mare.

SHADE

Early in the morning she entered the town through the Beautiful Gate. Wrapped in the coat of Venus. The roads were straight, the houses without roofs, the gardens angry with trees. Very soon she noticed, although she walked with the sun at her back, that there was no shade in the town. Those she asked explained to her: "Here, at dawn, we sweep everything in the sun's way that prevents it from being clean when it touches the ground." Towards mid-day she met an ass, standing in the middle of a square. As she was tired, she lay under the animal; so big was it that all the water from the town's wells could be poured into it. Those she asked explained to her that the ass was called, "Do not bring the shade upon us," and that it stood in the middle of the square so that no one would be made pregnant by the shade. And bear it children. Because this was the Sun's town and was to remain his. Then she knew she had reached the end of her journey. Longer than the darkness. And she pronounced a verdict: "I am the stone and here are the keys to open the door of the house you will build on me. In the house, make a bed for the ass of golden straw, so that he will feed with me."

ARABESQUE

Aga Mirak painted birds and flowers, water and the ruler. It was only she who alone was allowed to sleep in the ruler's bed that he was not allowed to paint. They would castrate him. He painted and painted the arabesques, millimeter after millimeter he covered with paint the images he drew and birds and flowers and water awoke in them — only the ruler's face alone could no more be traced. He painted for months, persistently, in the early mornings only, when the workers and the ruler were asleep. And then one morning, on the third day of the sixth month at dawn, the arabesque was finished; and it was her, they would castrate him because of her image. He fell asleep over her, exhausted, with his face on her belly, scratched by the ruler's ring. At that moment the ruler awoke and in the bed beside him was a painted arabesque in the shape of a flowery maze in the heart of which she was forever lost, she who alone was allowed to lie in his bed.

First she was summoned by the power of earth, so she went and wanted to fly. As if she heard a voice: "If you are of earth, step on me and help yourself." Then she crashed. A cold-blooded being, riding only with the sunny wind. Built in the palace of the north. And lo, the curtain in the temple tore in two, and she returned to the boy's feet. They said to the calendar: "Let this be the day of return." Some days after the night when he was to be born, she measured the falsified freedom for the last time and closed her eyes, which started to dry. For three days they were coming to see her, guessing whether she was still alive. On the fourth day, a thin pink line appeared on her belly. The boy pleaded: "Take her away from under my bed. I do not want to sleep with death." And he did not say: "Why did you leave me? I gave you the name." Even though he drank water through a straw; water, with which they could test if she was still alive. They did not gather beside her for some time. As if they had heard a message coming from her: "Do not look at me, do not guess about me, do not ask about my soul. It will scale off me and scatter in the middle of the room into the dust, so that the sun will always be seen in it." No more did they put food for her on the sand, they observed her secretly and looked into her departing eyes. And at the being, flaring up under the shield, where the light had imprinted its child-like fingers. "Father, I am putting her into your hands," said the body. And they waded through snow up to their knees as they carried her, wrapped in the sour tobacco smell, and covered her in dried excrement, to the bush. So that she burns. So that the cold compresses the bloody crack on her belly, with which the voice of earth called to it. So that the poor greenery calls her back. In the April of the hatched lark. They trembled as they returned to the snow-filled town.

EDUCATION

The severity of the period of education in the windy corridors of the house, named after gold and the number six — their language did not distinguish between the metal and the number — could only be compared to the dressage of wild horses. Needles, thrust into the pupils' elbows next to the veins, penetrated deeply at every wrong movement. Blood flooded the bright thin paper, on which they learned to inscribe his name. Under swallows' wings, the screams of pain of future scribes tore along the corridors. From cats' hairs, squirrels' fur and children's hair they bound brushes, thinner than the lashes of the first in the harem. Through straws, with warm inhalations, they lifted golden and silvery pigments from shells, and scattered the dust of his future name onto their papers. Spilt ink brought the whip with rusty nails upon the backs of the seated ones. Endlessly they copied the teachers' patterns of dragons, blooming trees, girls they would never see, and terrible rages living only in tales. Whipped a hundred times, his hands a hundred times numb, his veins perforated, his eyes dry, the best pupil received a precious gift before he was twelve. The first in the harem had not shaved her genitals for three months. During a solemn ceremony, before a stone veiled with black, before necks bent in prayer, she lifted her robe and pulled out six — which could also mean golden — young hairs, and placed them in the whipped boy's hand, which would henceforth write his name so that the name would be He himself.

SIYAVUSH

He was the first, with sunny skin, who knew that power was wooden iron. From the mountain, captured on the western march, when he was no bigger than the mountain eagle's egg. His sentences not only spoke, but also worked. Speech, which was work; words, houses, roads, bridges. He united three orthographies, he made love so quickly every night that blood never left his stomach. Of children he was as afraid as of knives, so he always, as it got dark, bound his scrotum. There was only one who was allowed to unbind the thin leather string, smelling of sweat and almond oil. The string, which she softly chewed, while he copulated into her, trembling; with sunny skin and the first, who knew that wooden iron holds the sceptre in an ignorant hand. Siyavush Georgian who united three orthographies.

126

BORIS A. NOVAK

CORONATION

1.

Memory has two wings: the first is past, the second is future.
Within us a poppy smelling grave is growing.
Where a space is too narrow to accept a step
Only voice can dwell in a dead bird's nest.

Our destiny is a freedom of language,
A high spell, a living blood from the time well.
The deep snow of centuries is waiting for us,
Dark of soot, washed out like a fragrant linen.

I am beginning the chant with a great praise to the milk.
A language of milk is whiter than absence.
Word is a womb of the human world.

This poem is beyond power and weakness: only a whisper
Kisses the mouth where the river is bound:
A luxury that hurts, a name of the silence.

2.

A luxury that hurts: a name of the silence.
There are fires and eyes burning everywhere.
Irrevocably alone, lost in a sweet confusion,
I am kissing hands to all the people; let it pass.

Let this luxury of the blue pass.
It is enough to be here once, at the edge
Between day and night, tracing signs of death.
The world is rich. I feel like dying of grace.

I have a left and a right hand.
With them I am building a nest for the shapes
of your body which is a sea and deep.

The ear is a shell of sounds and silence
In the sand of time sliding through my fingers.
Only dreams can weave time with water.

3.

Only dreams can weave time with water.
When everything familiar had strangely changed
A beautiful woman has thrown her shoes into a precipice
Tearing apart a night cobweb with her naked body.

A skirt is a wing shining lonely out of the deep.
(Who's traveling and where to? — Who's asking?)
The beginning of the end. And the end itself? Here it is:
A frightful poem, sister of the primordial silence.

Destiny is fulfilled exactly as light
In the morning and in the evening. And birds
Fleeing to the south pierce the presence.

Never more. Nowhere. Only little seeds,
Seeemingly dead, call the future time,
A magical mirror, a distant face of milk.

4.

A magical mirror: a distant face of milk,
Scarcely visible under the magnifying glass.
Sacred waters which haven't broken yet
Shield the fire with a silence of high priests.

When a woman's labor begins a laundress comes
To wash the sky in the light that streams away.
Blood has the strength of steel.
All things support each other like stairs.

The universe is open with a birth scream!
The body is a field — the wheat and sickle of the reaper.
Watch: a grain is growing into the highest image.

A trifling grain, smaller than the pupil of the eye,
The same in its desire for the name: the little is great.
Truth is always being born at the edge.

5.

Truth is always being born at the edge
Where an utterly sensitive seam
— The mouth of a river kissing a sea —
Is sewn with an invisible thread of the new language.

A prudent palm is making a childbed, celebrating
The body in the rhythm of a dream weaver.
Life is strained like the string on a bow —
On the spin of a sacred woman in labor.

Giving birth is a terrible gift for a woman.
But each and every thing is a tiny thread of a rug
That unites us all into the whole.

Only death undoes our weaving, making a hole
With scissors of emptiness. Under the earth our blood is green.
A child is building the whole world out of clay.

6.

A child is building the whole world out of clay.
For him the door is not just a birth of space —
It is the native space itself: the child has to
Open it to become a prince of the wide.

No wall can break time and space.
And the window is not just a bottomless eye
Of the wall — it is the precipice itself which has to
Be open by each child, each prince of the near . . .

The wardrobe hides an ancient treasure: childhood.
Hidden in folds of skirts, this fragrant,
Tiny, thrilling god will never die.

I've opened the door of my dusty homeland:
Magical tears. — Being grown up I am so poor.
A sand castle is stronger than emptiness.

7.

A sand castle is stronger than emptiness.
Invented and ruined by the movement of the moment,
Eternally ancient, it is being renewed and wasted again and again
Under fingers of each and every child, like a fruit.

An immense world is dripping through sensual sieves.
The nearest universe is open to be touched,
A mysterious skin is drinking air and sobbing
And hearing only the language of the moist and warm.

Senses wake up to play with colors and sounds.
A fateful bird of birth is nesting in time,
Filling an empty fist with a palmy kiss.

I am eating the world with an appetite of the spoonful.
The eyes of children are starving for things.
A mother eagle is shielding calls of the weak ones.

8.

A mother eagle is shielding calls of the weak ones.
Tender games of the beak with a fledgling
Are eternal rites at the peak of the mountain
Where earth rises high, high — to the knees of air.

When a woman carries a sunny seed of the message,
I'm just a man, confused and silent, witnessing
The creation of everything from a crack of nothing.
Her sex is the neck of a broken bottle.

With my palms I am trying to close the burning wound,

The utter sacrifice of the woman's body.
Her skin was never so naked!

Birth is a farewell hurting a child to scream!
We are beings of a bright, native solitude.
Anguish opens like a curtain.

9.

Anguish opens like a curtain.
This poem is a moment of silence just before a storm.
Gathering debris of the world torn apart.
Shielded by a wild rhythm I am dancing away from terror.

Mysterious memory is rising higher and higher.
A cypress above the open grave of history.
The sky is enlightened by falling stars,
Wheels of fire, nightmares from the dark childhood of time.

Look, a bulldog with a mouth full of bloody slaver!
When morning begins to mourn and the poem is a curse
And a city is a tower of glass and brass without pity,

Only a child rescues the space with his fresh eyes.
The child is a holiday, a day born out of a hole.
The child is a crown. I crown you, my life.

10.

The child is a crown. I crown you, my life.
The whole world is a modest throne for the infant king.
His smile is everything: the greatest hand of light,
Snow for us who are melting snowmen.

The child is created twice: by birth and by milk.
Breasts are sanctuaries of milky rituals nursing the universe,
The mouth of a sea into a new-born river.
The milk is a pure will, a living water of creation.

Being little the child is living near secrets: he knows by heart
Each and every wrinkle on the wooden face of the furniture.
For him every day is a birthday. A new continent to be discovered.

Only the corner of the eye is sensitive enough to see the weakest
Stars: when you watch them directly they vanish into
The densest moment — terrible is the gold of the body.

11.

The densest moment: terrible is the gold of the body,
An ore radiating into nothing, a grain in the flood.
How can a bow still find the color of the sound
Locked deep in the memory of the ear.

After the fire the darkness is still darker.
Future days, all those prophetic lights and lies,
Will collapse under the weight of the triumphal arch.
How to rescue a cradle from the earthquake.

A bloody rain will wipe out chalk marks on the blackboard.
A snowman will kill himself melting away.
Only poems still keep the word,

Drawing wings for children to fly.
How to build a house with the mere strength of the eye.
The blooming of the world demands a serene vigil.

12.

The blooming of the world demands a serene vigil.
In a poem I am someone who's always missing.
To make a verse sound perfect, I am silent.
To make a flower be perfect, I am fading away.

I am subtracted from the total of everything. — Time is friction. —
The result of the calculation is zero, without a remainder:
The body is a mortal weapon and a mortal wound. Vanishing,
My face is spellbound into the pure vibration of my voice.

I am withdrawing. Now you can watch the field through my ribs.
Nothingness makes me dangerous and vulnerable.
Every fist is full of a terrible will, so I make it a palm.
A change: step here, into the spell of our farewell,
Where I stand. I am no longer there. Instead of me there's a universe.
Here, my child, I bequeath to you all the wonders.

13.

Here, my child, I bequeath to you all the wonders.
I, a king of the language, am resigning to the rhymes
Of a royal insensibility, being hurt
By the word. The poem is a body of the body.

I am leaving to you all the eyes and strength of the tree,
Laps blossoming in the middle of winter,
Secrets to hide yourself and call me: I'm not here,
Treasures of sounds and this key of the ear.

I am writing to you with the blue ink of the deep
Where waters of time fall down in a foam.
Don't be afraid. I am a bridge over the fear of heights.

But every peak is a slippery threshold into emptiness.
Don't be afraid — I won't let the world crash the silence of
The knees where I cradle you into floating.

14.

The knees where I cradle you into floating
Are flourishing, full of milk, full of nothing.
The lullaby is a soft, sonorous lid
Slowly covering your dreams. Go away, fears.

Learning to rise you're bigger than life.
And you fall down. An immense river always washes away
The world while you're running to become a man
In order to stop the spinning of the earth.

But between yourself and death there is my body
Guarding you. When birds are bound to burn
Only man is free to sing.

Absence will drink out all my eyes.
When you grow up, whisper to this poem: You are mine.
Memory has two wings: the first is past, the second is future.

SONNET OF SONNETS

Memory has two wings: the first is past, the second is future,
A luxury that hurts, a name of the silence.
Only dreams can weave time with water:
A magical mirror, a distant face of milk.

Truth is always being born at the edge:
A child is building the whole world out of clay —
A sand castle is stronger than emptiness.
A mother eagle is shielding calls of the weak ones.

Anguish opens like a curtain.
The child is a crown. I crown you, my life.
The densest moment: terrible is the gold of the body.

The blooming of the world demands a serene vigil.
Here, my child, I bequeath to you all the wonders,
The knees where I cradle you into floating.

STILL LIFE AND DEATH

The fame is undressing a candle and the light is dressing
a room where mirrors reflect each other
and trembling eyes of fire run away
from the immobility of glass deep into the glass infinity.

The voice of a bird is raining from the open cage of time,
and echoing among shadows of shadows,
and dying at the edge of hearing and silence;
in the corner absent fingers are playing the guitar.

In reflecting corridors a woman is flowing,
tender as snow and alive as a melody;
when her skin wants to be fulfilled in a touch
she kisses only her own image, cold and distant.

And nothing happens between eyelashes and timelashes;
and nothing does happen: silent happening of nothingness.
Thus the still life is translated into a still death,
the woman into a desire and the desire into the thirst of language.

POEM

A poem is not a world: it is a pure word,
a birth of the language and a language of the birth in the womb of silence.
The poem is not a thing: it is a child of every-thing and no-thing.

The poem is not a light: it is a will for light,
not a fire, but a key of the fire hidden in the night.
The poem is not a woman: it is a silent desire, an embrace of rhymes.

The poem is not a music: it is a naked voice snowing
from the blue sky of hearing to the ceiling of the feeling,
memory of meaning about its childhood so full of sounds.

The poem is not an image: it is a magical mirror.
The poem is not a letter: not by me, it is written by the language itself,
and not to you, it is addressed to everybody and nobody.

And the poem is not a poem: it is the meaning of a meadow and the meadow of
                                            memory,
memory of the body and the body of no-body: the poem is when it is not: sand:
a seed of the unspeakable growing in the paper grass of nothingness, without a
                                            point.

WINTER

Winter is a time frozen to total whiteness.
White is the path, white the pathfinder, white the finding of the void.
Silence is white, yet I can not shade it, for my voice is whiter.
The light is a soft, white silk; the world is a beautiful white corpse . . .

But whence so much whiteness? From the white sky.
The horizon? A fiction; unmeasurable, unspeakable whiteness,
no more: whiteness with no bound, no peak, no bottom,
a painful mystery, the first and last . . .

White grass in the fields. Trees with white leaves.
White sheep in a white sleep. Black wolves howling white.
Clouds in a white sky — white, bright, insane stains!
White roofs on houses; inside them, a whitened fear . . .

White is the water captured in icy chains:
white the waterfall trapped in mid-air; white the river with no ripples.
White, and void, and beautiful the canvas of the winter scene.
White and cold, and warm the blanket of the earth as it sleeps, sleeps, sleeps . . .

White, white are the games: children are snowballs among snowballs —
those little masons building a skyscraper of ice,
those little pilots flying on wooden sleds,
those little sculptors cutting one-day snowmen . . .

White, white, white is your body! . . . The icy mirror
of the water's surface steals away your white beauty.
Whiteness is scraping beneath our steps. — We are running out of time! —
The only warmth in this white cold is your white hot hand . . .
The sky's volcano vomits snow; the eye is blinded by white lava.
An avalanche is just a curl falling from the mountain's old white head.
A white storm wipes out our trails . . . Only a chimney writes with black ink,
but the horizon — a white sponge — erases its smoky writing . . .

It snows . . . white rice at the wedding of the sky and earth, sled of dreams.
It snows . . . pulverized whiteness, milk to nurse a child's eye:
a boy is melting ice from the window with a breath warm of amazement —
and falling whiteness makes him fly, fly, fly high into the sky . . .

A white wind erases space into a pure whiteness, a white peace.
Days are short, nights are long, both are white: time is white.
(I write to blaze a trail through this winter, white, void paper;
but no use: white are the words, these beautiful words with no traces . . .)

This whiteness wiping out all the traces . . . this is time snowing within us.
This snow covering all the tracks . . . this is death living within us. —
Under its white winter crust a deathbearing river brings a new time:
new springs and summers for us . . . and a whole eternity without us . . .

MILAN JESIH

from VOLFRAM

Unseen angels walk noiselessly — barefoot without stirring the wind — around the sleeping houses; this is now. Wooden I lie awake in *didaskalia*, my eyes weary, mouth dry, with a heart that knows everything: everything, when even nothing was too much. The merciless hour of sheets — the date gone, impressing no memory of its traces. Just like those angels outside leaving no footprints in the grass. Bread is melting in the cupboard. On chandeliers flies are lulled into a light sleep. I, too: just to fulfill the longing of my eyelids! To slide into sleep!

But there are no angels: it is I who unknowingly stumble in blind images around neighbors, scenting their wives and daughters instead of being in my room; let all of me fall asleep, rest my eyes and give dreaming wings to my bubbling blood. The heart knows everything (when even nothing was too much), but is still fond of pounding: perhaps this is the only true way of being. This is now: the cherry branch in the vase is locked in a spawning of time; on the table cooked spinach, made for the noon meal, hovers in water.

Tonight I again stared at the moon: hastened to meet her on the way to a pub, followed her on my way home. On the foothills shone, like sugar crystals, houses between barren trees, the people in them have fallen into their honorable sleep; wine was pounding inside me, and if a soul were anywhere awake, I'd have knocked and stolen some affection: but even the dogs were quiet. I was wading in time; in my pupils the spell of an unknown night as if I were a pious man, kneeling in some cathedral.

I stepped into my room kneeling. Turned on the light. Swept photographs on the wall with a glance. Oh, gracious thanks! on the table, solitary, white, where from! alone! from merciful nymphs given an apple: let the teeth, grown for a candid laugh, bite into it, the teeth I no longer have, let then the mouth be happy; I halted on my knees by the door, fingers of my stretched hand on the doorknob at the height of my shoulders: an embryo in an unnatural, dangerously abortive position.

The city quarter of Sentvid is golden — washed by a rainstorm, made serene by the sun's brightness,
calmed by a fresh wind from the Gorenjska fields. The soul, likewise, longs to rest:
I sit by the window with a sleeping book in my arms, lost in the dark blue of the sky, too shy to get up,
tired of sitting, melancholic after reading the lives made into literature. Sunk in thoughts: my mother believed
everything was predestined, I've insisted that man chooses for himself and therefore

I kept putting off a great deal of time for some future time — and it so happened that my present self
and my future self stayed awake for some fat years. Now there is nothing promising or encouraging, the heart freed
from the weight of a hopeless hoping: it is time to turn the TV on, foreign wars and the long legs of sniper guns,
and simply be. To chase the corrosion out of the heart, though — who can tell? The air is soft, each breath grace:
Oh, clouds! Lambs that escaped to the sky! Aided by winds, kind brothers, they reached the heights of their dreams!

The night is dark and silent. Only when a shy south wind blows, the open window winces and the dancer in the curtain pleats stirs. The night is a dark solitaire, deep like a grave and as gently inviting, softly luring: it kneads doubt into the heart dough, filling people's bodies with anxiety, and they desire to escape out, across currant bushes and gardens, across streets, bridges and meadows, through mountains crushed to scree, over straits and birch trees — away into a freshly-dug distance;

the evil steals itself into everything, gnawing the skin, corroding metals — utter destruction is its measure: even when for a moment a tiny flame begins to shine in a rat in a cellar or an insect in pea blossoms, a flame that is hope and faith, it hunts it down and kills it. The air in the room is humid, scentless, without memory — its presence a shuddering touch to eyelids. With a blanket wrapped around my knees I sink into an armchair and wish to remain that way, frozen in time.

When a tiger sheds its skin — how vulnerable becomes its flesh! — a blanket will embrace me like crust, harsh, dry, sleep with a face of promise will take me in: when an animal sheds its skin, when the air is expansive on a plain, how full of death the room becomes! Who was I? White distances, savage naked beauty, an intense presence, bubbling miracle, an inspired will — thirty years of childhood, much pathos and milk and — ho! — the terrifying unfulfillment of man!

And so what? Should wars start so I'll pull myself together? And have, ashen from fear, one wish only: to live? Or an unexpected love in Italy. Or snails, slithering in the moist garden. Or coal in cellars. It is not true that the sound of an accordion is heard in times like such. Nothing is heard. Nothing is there. I smell of sweat. My shirt, my wrist watch and weights. No manifestations of change: everything remains in its assigned, improper place.

I have arrived and it is true: the house has neither the teeth of a sea-urchin nor the hopes of wives rebelling against their husbands: the blossoms of the hallway are opening, the weight of rain is foreign, left outside. Here there is only the good old sameness: the halted thought of an angel and traces of the fragrance of hay. What, then, do I bring: not a gift or letter in my hands, not a heart or star inside my chest: just some barefoot words behind my ear — I put my T-shirt on and between drinking and salvoes, without a shade of distance,

I watch spellbound — as if in oblivion, or in devastation, or some different, distant life — a small table made of black rosewood, encrusted with copper, on it three napkins, three teaspoons, cacao in three little cups: oh! the interior so tranquil in a stable charisma and enchanted symmetry, leaving me breathless, opiated, removing past and future lives as the fragile rain rustles behind young curtains like the divination of a prophet.

My writing eluded me, I was absent-minded, the paper is now full of an unrecognizable scribbling,
a new order is rising all around me: butterfly curtains on the windows, tapestries on the walls, rugs on the parquet floor,
and on the ceiling a horoscope in which the glowing beings of heaven tremble quietly; Aries shot Sagittarius,
Aquarius is throwing Pieces on Libra (it all happens in tranquility), Scorpio dies lying on Virgo, Gemini have escaped,
they are gone — strangely resembling the truth?

I should put my skates on and in one leap cut the planet to pieces; who knows what is holding me back.
"The skate is hard to put on." "The ice is so wooden." "This house has no door." " I'm not going anywhere today."
Kneeling in the middle of the room I am shivering; was there a need for all this?
No gravitation, no magnetism, no powers — just the alien presence of my native world without hope
and without reminiscence: a hand holding a hand like an unknown wet glove.

At night, when birds are asleep, there are stars the birds don't know of unless they open their eyes from the pain of dreams. Night is a soft discreet charm: luring is the playful pliable hour — offering, but in truth taking, bringing tears smilingly; and how it showered itself with flowers! and the gentle wind; its mane, adorns its nape, spoiled by kisses! and the tempting siren-like silence, the night's magic spell which is killing, killing everything, and iron and the pristine pagan faith!

The birds are oblivious to this and to the stars unless they open their eyes from the pain of their dreams and stare, bewildered, into the night. They don't know of me digging ceaselessly inside myself to find a memory that would console me, forgetting I am not a mine. Then, what am I? A huge blueberry, full of sharp human horror; distance and promise; and the birds don't know, the birds are asleep. They know nothing unless they open their eyes from the pain of their dreams as a cold shiver awakens the soft cores of their hearts.

This unknown village — strewn on the slope as if it wished to climb the mountain — this village is my home. My heart knows its church-bells, its apple-trees in blossom, the old men and women and their south seas, their northern fears. It was there I experienced all the big things of my childhood: my father's joke, the clear laughter of my mother, a headless rooster, matches in a hayloft and all the things and thoughts permeated with a healthy ardent anticipation.

Distances, distances. Now I sit in the brittle library of a dark foreign city, my blood throbbing lazy and lethargic in my temples. The village! maidens are rocking their breasts under thin linen, while I have deliberately chosen the bare life, denounce everything to quench my thirst for learning, so I'd not stay small in myself; a pearly honey has gathered around my pain, passions evaporate after being stirred by the forceful winds of time— and afterwards we don't know how it all was or what the life was all about.

Morning, a graceful morning arose amidst the mountaintops; no force can hold back the fragility of time in its awakened trepidation; like nothing can hold back the growth of day, the opulence of light; and what has rotten in the heart cannot be brought back to life: all through the night — an intense new moon in May — I was writing a poem: of my heart's desire for joy, affection and trust. But, I gave birth to pain: my poem became a vessel of distress, and the shards of my broken life are now staring at me.

The world is asleep, faces peaceful; if not for their likeness to blossoms I'd think they were dead. My fingernails hurt from the lazy passing of minutes, grating my trembling: I am a human bomb, a scream of despair! The forest is oblivious to ants and people: everything ever coming to life in it will return from the same into the same. I spread honey on bread, milk is boiling, I take a clean napkin; an immense drop of the sun's light floods the shadows of earth.

JURE POTOKAR

WELLS AND OTHER DEPTHS

you are untouchable as the image etched out
by a laser. even the white-hot shouts of a mob
can't reach you. you grow whiter,

more absent, glassy. like the eye of an exhausted
deer fleeing before a raging fire. you'll never
get beyond the edges marked by silver

moonlight and its chill, sharper
than the broken skin of a snow-draped swamp.
through the heavy skeins that silence knots you again

catch sight of what was once within your reach.

NIGHTS WITH NO MORNING

in your habitat there is no space for human
voices or the electric pull that bodies
have. your tongue is lame from endless grief.

for you silence is just a remedy for defeats
which fatalism has turned into the echo
of a curse long since pronounced.

you've fastened metal bars onto your door,
their cool green saps the warmth from your hands.
only the clock lives undisturbed, marking time and waiting

for the arrival of the god who chose solitude for you.

WAITING

again we've reached a time for waiting, a time of subsidence,
when the pulsing in the veins is scarcely felt,
yet keeps on going.

the world is focused in a single dot, a point frozen still,
for it perceives its goal through decades and knows it.
o, waiting, man's favorite brand of certainty.

THEIR GENIUS

they're waiting for you, haven't even moved the chairs,
only their eyes roam the walls, which even now are
lit by a single, small kerosene lamp.

its chimney is sooty, so much that the flame
barely shows. the wick is too long, as ever, but
no single chair creaks, and a hand moves.they're still

waiting for you, for your hand, destined to do this the best way.

TOUCHING

you've left with a body that has passed into memory, like
a nomad's dwelling that layers and layers of sand
bury with unmatched persistence. bitter, barely discernible,

yet so final. you'll count, and with intolerable
clarity, perhaps, make out a coin ringing against
cement, snow falling softly into the November nights.

you'll be alone in this listless time of bitter colors,
where there is no space for irony, alone among
bloodthirsty smells of times gone by, alone and in company

thinking of a touch that will never again be yours.

ANATHEMA

I don't trust that deeply in myself, nor do I trust
that deeply in changes *outside* myself. all these syllables
withering on soaked paper are just a pretense,

clumsy attempts at exact definition, as we know.
the anathema has been pronounced, become a cry
whose resonance confirms the power and persistence of the cold

within numbed selves, where it's meant to flourish.
afterwards how calm I am, loquacious in my solitude,
and how belief wanders in and out of the cobwebbed church.

yet I don't trust that deeply in myself. for that the stone's too hard.

PEACOCK

it draws in one leg a bit, and your skin, too,
has stopped being that significant, weightless softness.
what's really missing remains to be found.

though it may altogether be just a vague foreboding.
I found the stretch of beach, no problem, and your footprints
are still there, though slightly eroded from long waiting

for that final wave that will tell them the truth of your departure.

AFTER A DEFEAT

after a defeat your movements are more guarded.
it's hard to stop the fissures that let the cold
seep through your bleached, divided self.

yet, blind endurance drags on. the words
you've spoken have exposed only you, and this
is why silence can so often be such balm,

the counterpart to gusts of air in a broken flute
as it gathers speed. in silence's carminic shadings
you lose your warm breath, and the capillaries in you

burst with such a strange and wonderful sound.

TOUCH

folds of skin shine through the stiffness of shapes, and messages
bent and straightened, supple from warmth or cold and sharp
drip toward them through the cuts. a contact nestling

in subsurface regions that wanders through repeated callous
interludes into a maze. we dissolve distances
through touching, a scratch at softness and trickle through

each other's armor. at the center the miracle of feeling shines
like enamel whiteness. *touch* is memory's unicorn, another world
astray in sharpness, that flares up in a tiny spot when we knead it

with our fingertips and the gift of enduring responds.

A VOICE

in that ether forces rage unknowable to us,
there is no light, not even the gleam of cats' eyes,
you just hear a voice emptily echoing.

that voice sends shivers through your down,
sets the eardrums banging in a precarious rage,
a rhythm you've anticipated many years,

but which eludes your attempts to observe it.
this voice, these subtle tremors of air, such that dust
settles and evades your cupped hand gliding through it.

RURAL LOVE I

they come in the evenings
to stand around in the inn,
with beer at the bar
they drink with the guys.

only when it gets late
do they liven up, their avid
gulps wipe the day
from their glistening eyes.

they touch the girls
secretly, late in
the night the arms around
the shoulder squeeze more tightly.

up from their collars
a male smell forces its way.
their palms are moist
and rough.

they drive their girls
home by car,
they are preoccupied as
the desire for their quarry grows.

RURAL LOVE II

if he has waited for you a few times,
brought you home
pleasantly and politely,
if he has talked to your father,

then you must put together the dowry,
they've said, for sure, there'll be
an engagement and some kids,
with any luck.

what he hasn't said to you
you work out for yourself,
and you don't go to dances
any longer.

you clear out all the old
dolls and junk
from your room. that's where
the marriage bed should be.

you hope it's not a mistake,
you are often absorbed in thoughts,
alone between the walls
you tremble within yourself.

LATE SUN

you burned
the path
scarlet,
burned through the field,
sting-point of the sky.

across you
flames
splashed
sand-drifts of dark,
salty waters.

scorching
over the half-orb
they seethed,
extinguished you,
evaporated.

so that the gulls
took flight,
when you
were drowning them
in fire.

WHEN IT IS TIME

when it is time I set my chair by the door
and count the mosquitoes in the air, early in the morning
I disturb the turkeys and encounter a blue-colored bird
in the hollow of the road, and also chase off the eagles
with my shouting. as soon as it is September
I fight with the mist, but never with the sun.
I point out the paths to anyone who comes,
then occupy space again in that place.

MOTHER

when early in the morning
she gets up
and quietly shuts
the door behind her,
I occasionally
hear her
and wrap myself
in my sheets,
still half asleep.

from my misty dreams
arise the outlines
of the buildings, the barn,

I look,
I know
she's working.

at the table
I meet her and the smell of the barn.
in her hands
still rests the coolness
of the cold morning
water,
of the drink for the animals.

I am dumb
as her calloused palm
touches
the dishes
and cleans them
from the table.

FARM MOTHER AND DAUGHTER

she says:
you'll hear our story all over again now.
she thinks:
she should leave now so it won't be too hard on her.
she says:
let me bake some fruit bread for you.
she thinks:
at least she'll take away something nice to remember us by.
she asks:
did you get the letter at all.
she thinks:
I waited a long time to see her, really too long.

the girl nods,
afraid of the unspoken thoughts.
in their hearts
two birch-trees could grow.

AHEAD INTO WORSE TIMES

I shall go,
when the father's houses
will be growing old,
when the long corridors
will be open.

squeezed beneath
the silent threshold
I shall search for myself
for thousands of days.

there will come days
of copper in the hair,
iron in the eyes,
when in my own
memory I shall not
recognize myself,
diffirent even
before myself.

FEAR

I breathe in
and hold my breath,
in on myself
I am huddled.

fearfully
through the door,
I clutch the handle
to find out
if it is shut fast
behind me.

then I breathe out
and again breathe in,
perhaps there is still someone
behind the door.

I take a look
and I know there is no one.

bewildered,
pressed close to myself
in the iron-and-concrete building
alone
out into the narrow
undeafened night
I slide.

I HAVE WALKED

I have walked
after days without peace
full of words of ill repute
in among the larches.

the earth
this day has been
bloated with clammy heat.

prespiring and
breathing heavily
I am aware
that I am walking on and on.

in a clearing
I wrap myself
in the smell of pitch,
I pick a full fist
of strawberries,
with my mouth full
I sit through till evening,
happy as beetles
in spring.

NOTHING REMAINS

nothing remains of the illusion of security, which settles like a sickness in the
memory and persists, impatient. the endless knot here, so that I am at a loss for words,
the elevator of the year descends to a hallway too low and the vineyards
outside recall the place. impermanence has seized the walls and the innuendoes.

total alarm veils the audacious charm: anew I choose among the phantoms of home
and abroad, and attempts at domestication come to naught in flight. I note the ancient
grievance and the idea of the experience of weakness, as if it could not increase,
and remembrance is shortened into the fleeting sensation that the microbes are
                                                                trembling.

MY CAUTIOUS COMING

my cautious coming into the world forces me into embarrassment, no longer can
I bewitch despair with a gentle thought, no longer do I try to destroy events in
my head. the end awaits immensely, and nonchalant movements in the makeshift
dwelling-place here erase the impressions. I am sober as never before.

and what I said will need mending. all the visible and previous days have gathered
in a motley cumulus and what have I not sketched with glances into the single
                                                                significance
of time with the idea of happiness! o, final irresponsibility, neither deceiving
nor corrupting. the watery mosaics are surging everywhere. I am entering I enter.

THERE ARE DAYS

there are days when tapestries are hanging in the town for the curious Japanese and
platinum lights shimmer like silver over the entrances. there is a time when memory
comes from the promised land quite absently and deceptively, and death is cool only
when touched. the day is all jagged, trampled, and there is no plea for life.

there are cramped times when I choose incarnate stupidities anywhere, I approach on
                                                                tiptoe,
I swallow them and would believe something of it all: the singing, the sentence which
deserves to be reconciled a bit later and becomes numb with repetition. sensuous is
the god whom I have wooed and who, with opium lips, makes fun of the orphan, of
                                                                anyone.

159

ALOJZ IHAN

THE SIXTH DAY

I know, the fifth night is when the doubts come,
and unpleasant dreams, for everything is done, everything
set into motion, and then and there You realized that
one day Your stars would be left without light,
that Your sun would cool, and the plants
would wither, the animals die, for
no being come from the world is created
for a dark sun, for the cold, and endless aloneness,
for suffering, and no way out. And when You saw
that one day amid all this You would again be left
all alone, terrified, on the sixth day, You grabbed for the clay.

THE SEASONS

Lips in a pout, she blew
the hair off her forehead. There! That
was what stirred him most, time and again. But
he never told her. Perhaps he was afraid that
it might change then. Be gambled away forever.
Nor did he ever show it. He only looked on,
and his heart hammered away. Sometimes she didn't do it
the whole day long. Sometimes she waited a week.
Muggy summers were the exception. Winters,
he made sure the apartment steamed
from the heat. Spring and fall he didn't like.
He remembered that he had once waited
all of March and half of April.

161

MEDITATION: AFTERNOON

It is afternoon and nobody who has been walking
since morning can now return.
Many a man will have to sleep in a stranger's
hayloft or on the grass or on the damp
ground. Bewildered, many a one will
listen-in all night on the forest voices or
suddenly note on his neck the cold
slithering of a snake. Many a one will then
bolt into panicky flight or
sob helplessly into his hands till morning. And
maybe the happiest people really are those
who every evening realize anew
that all day long they were walking around in circles.

OF THE UNKNOWN BATTLE

which does not appear in history textbooks nor
in children's stories, of which the papers
do not write, about which the radio and
television reporters keep quiet, though every
day a river washes up a body from somewhere,
or a body dangles from a branch, or somebody bleeds to death
out an artery in the neck or lies fallen, smashed to bits,
at the foot of a highrise and the people surround him,
the dead soldier, the fallen comrade, whom nobody
will cover with a flag and play the anthem for,
though they all secretly know that in reality
the battle is bloody and this might have been their best
bomber or sharpshooter that has just foundered and henceforth
each victory will be more difficult to come by and every hope
fainter.

THE DANCE

Secretly, they're also afraid, the children, puzzled
by the wild merriment, and the men, with
their shovel-like hands breaking the waists of women, and
the women, trapping the wind neath their skirts that
birdlike they might fly, and stretching their arms to the sky,
their pupils milky from the stars and blind
to light; secretly, they're afraid, the children,
who feel the start of an ecstasy and search for the movement
which will make their equilibrium waver, and search for the word
which will cast a spell over everything; secretly, they're afraid,
the children, until the innkeeper looks at the clock and
they watch how everything must be put back in its place
when the music dies down and the musicians put
their fiddles away, the women must straighten their dresses,
the men must put their hands back in their pockets
or on their bottles, all words spoken in the heat of passion
must become sweet jests, and only some drunk is permitted
to dream all night long until morning, when the sweepers
awake and erase every last trace.

TORNADO

The street was empty and the windows nailed shut, everybody
was indoors waiting for the tornado, gathered around
the television which was showing how,
with its huge ringed belly, it was nearing the city,
how, like a confused drunkard, it was grabbing hold
of trees and houses and then disappointedly throwing them
into the air like so many inedible mushrooms. It entered the city
with a boom, like entering a large drugstore,
the screens tinkled from the storefronts
it was playfully touching and breaking like soap bubbles,
then the satellite picture came on
and everybody could see nicely how
the vacuumed streets, smoothly, like spaghetti,
slid into the whirling gullet. The natives knew
the names of all the streets and murmured them

163

through gritted teeth, the newcomers could do the same
only when the vortex took the nearer neighborhood in,
then the screen went out
just before the people might have seen
their very own street slip away, just before
they might have caught in the magic mirror
their own face and eyes, their terrifying depths,
which are ready any moment to give away
like the deceptive membrane of the birth sac, just before
their last simple message, before the end, the way
it always happens to people, their bedtime prayer
dies down to a whisper, then the angels take it up, whom
none of the sleeping can still distinguish from their dreams.

OF HUMAN FLESH

I rebelled, everyone in the group rebelled.
The guide explained to us that cannibalism
was in these parts an age-old, disturbing
tradition, and that the meal would remain
in our fondest memories. As to the flesh, he promised
it would be fresh, wholesome and very young,
indeed, a child's, and that there would be nothing
illegal in this as the child had died
a natural death, from hunger. Moreover, the agency paid
the parents or relatives an exceptionally high price,
and thus, with every bite, we would, in effect,
be making possible one whole meal for another hungry
child and, thus, perhaps, be saving him from death. From
that day on, I have been eating human flesh.

THE BOY IN THE TREE

For Edvard Kocbek

Then they begin to search for him. Torches aflame,
people scatter through the forest
calling out his name. Boatmen
take to the lake and sink
their poles into its murky depths. The dogs
are let loose from their chains. The boy squats
in the tree and watches in distress.
A little while longer and he'll hear the weeping,
the bells will ring, out of the house
a prayer will sound. Then the boy will slide
stealthily down from his tree
and, comforted now, head
for the precipice.

LITTLE SOLDIER OF THE BIG ARMY

Little soldier of the big army, don't be afraid,
your war will be won, you cannot make
a mistake so big that you could lose it, and defeated
will the soldiers of the little armies be, they cannot
perform heroics grand enough to be victorious;
don't be afraid, little soldier of the big army,
proudly will you march down the streets of captured
cities, on the highest steeples will you hang your
flags, in taverns the frightened waiters
will commandeer for you the best tables, and the beautiful
foreign women will answer to your slightest gesture;
no one will ever force you to flee, and you will be used
only to victories, always, as long as you are a little soldier
of the big army, so don't be afraid, your war will be won,
you cannot make a mistake so big that you could
lose it, and defeated will the soldiers of the little armies be,
they cannot perform heroics grand enough to be
victorious; don't be afraid, little soldier of the big army!

LOVER

Then she closes her eyes. Her eternal lover
bends over her, kisses her, and the woman
returns his kiss; then they stroke, provoke,
seize one another; the woman suddenly feels him inside her
and happily gives herself up to him, over and over, and slips into spasm
then her eternal lover slowly rises, takes his farewell,
is leaving, and the woman smiles to him; in a little while
she opens her eyes, beside her lies a man's
naked body; the woman rises and goes
into the bath.

ALEŠ DEBELJAK

NORTHERN ELEGIES

Earth. Red earth. And tall grass as far as you can see. You're pressed to the ground. Hidden from unwanted glances. Utterly still. A quail by your ear. Are you turning into stone? No: you're just listening to shadows fall over cornfields. A bead of sweat — a tear? — slides down your cheek. In the distance a mountain rises steeply. Naked. Without trees or flowers. Imprinted on the sharp-edged horizon. On its peak, lost in the clouds, generations of stag-hunters wander for centuries. Glistening of the setting sun. All the signs say: end of Indian summer. If I hear it right, nothing comes from your lips. Are you dumb? Blind? Perhaps you're searching through memory for the shapes of all prints — footsteps in the snow, old songs and cognac in the evening, small white towns with castles and turrets, the smells of Sunday afternoons, the river running under granite bridges. As if this, too, escapes you. Here, under the empty sky of ancient tribes you never heard about, you'll end your way. I, of course, always return. You don't. Which makes all the difference.

*****

The sodden moss sinks underfoot when we cross half-frozen bays and walk through birch groves, wandering in an uneven circle that widens into darkness, through the minds and bodies of men and animals trapped in last year's snow —no: trapped from the beginning, emptiness all around us, ice collecting on our pale faces, I can hear you singing on the run, an unknown melody, I can't make out the words, clouds of breath freeze on your fur collar, eyes open wide as we trudge through silence and weakening starlight, through the fevered babble of children exiled to distant camps, insects curling up under bark, December or June, no difference, ashes blanket the ground as far as you can see, damp wool of

167

shirts, we wade through the fog rolling in from the hills, oozing into our lungs, hills where there must be flowers about to bloom under a woman's eyelids, who dreams of dark faces hardening into granite, the snow's covering us, we're asleep on our feet, under the steel-grey sky, oblivious to the rhythms of sunrise and sunset, endless, as if they never began, our teeth crack in the cold, we don't want to separate, I can barely swallow, tell me the lyrics of your song, I want to sing with you.

*****

Horses sculpted in black marble. In town swept by gusts of winter wind. Rip themselves off their pedestals? No: perhaps they're tempted to go with the boy. The one who woke this morning, serious and dizzy. Woke from sleep overrun by a faint image, blurring. His companions try to keep him from leaving right away. He walks in silence toward the North. Across wheat fields, through birch groves. He won't rest till he reaches the glacier. While he ages like wine. Will he return? Eskimos lead him safely through snowfields and over the Bering Strait. In their boats he sleeps easily. Like anyone would: this is his home. Not that he would erase memory. Only in the glint of frozen water, in crystals and smooth ice does day become bitter enough for him. Only one move — and what was once solid disappears. The only thing that lasts is the careless flow of time. In the dreams of other men the boy looks calmly over the dark backs of horses and knows what I don't know how to say. Others would need a lifetime. Today, tomorrow, yesterday: it's all the same. I, too, will do what I should have done long ago.

*****

In this moment, in the twilight of a cold room, thunder approaches from a distance through storm windows and dusty panes, in late afternoon, the water in the pot doesn't boil, when fish gasp under the ice, when half-asleep you tremble, as if without hope, when a pack — a herd of shivering stags left the dried marshes deep in the woods and came to the gardens in the town, this fleeting instant, when the cold slices through your spine, when hardened honey cracks in jars, when the thought of a woman's hand — laid on the forehead of the dying — comes closer and closer, when from the depths of memory destroyed villages you wanted to forget begin to rise, when guilt and truth burn your stomach, when frightened pheasants are flushed from tapestries hanging on the wall, when guards leaving their posts whistle to one another piercing the air, when a sharp

168

stone breaks your skull, should I remind you now that your wounded
body won't be any different than the shadow a solitary bush casts across
the trampled earth, east of Eden?

*****

Your story's simple. You won't see many loved ones when you return, like
an otter surfacing in a lake to catch its breath. You won't find words for
short greetings, the seasons, unsuccessful missions, white phosphorus
lighting the passion in soldiers' eyes, a distant whistle on steep hillsides
you never climbed, children's cane baskets floating silently across a river
basin, the way you have a constant burning pain, the constellations
discovered in a premonition, Oriental love songs, the disappointment of
everything we were and will be. Believe me: this is your story. Later, I'll
tell it again — only better.

THE CATALOG OF DUST

I

Over the leaf of a thin paper runs a crack. A weather vane turns
gently in the eternal circle of the day; everything ever written
is already evaporating in four directions. — He, who now watches
the marsh blossom, sees the seed and decanting of juices. Sees

everywhere the shore and the sea that might not exist. In his eyes
the suburbs of New Orleans grow red. Sees somebody, who was poisoned
to his bones by sadness. He will, on the dusty surface of a wine
glass, watch with melancholy a pale silhouette. Distinguishing it

from anxiety and violence, from the song of a nightingale, from
parchment meditations, from selfishness and impatience. He won't return
what he hasn't taken. He'll measure love and the volume of eternity. —He,
who watches now, sees a woman with a dark spot in the softness of her back.

169

II

It appears like a smooth marten fur, leaping from the undergrowth
into an anguished omen. No muffled thundering of horned owls can be
heard. Things are going into hiding, evermore. A bitter juice from
snake-grass deepens the wound as it runs over it.

On the border between East and West a fox is barking into a sweetish
night. Over a pillow some woman's hand is searching for kisses of
the times past. Time is ticking off in a wrist watch. The atmosphere
is bleeding from all the above. As if this image would depend

on somebody who is also frightened. Spellbound people watch
intently how a straight line shoots up from the east side,
penetrating bread, almond seeds and cornea.
This, too, has been written down before.

III

Today will not be different from other days. He will nurse
his boredom and renew the botany from the brief afternoon dreams.
He will stand by the window curtain, longer than usual. He will
open the shutters, look towards the town squares, the streets,

and into a May dusk. In the dust of a garden he will, for an instant
or two, see a stag. Stalked by a soldier. The temperature in his
brain will rise, behind his back he'll probably hear a saxophone
player practising for a gig. As if by coincidence a shiver will run

down his spine. He'll feel the taste of cheap rum in his throat.
He'd like to believe everything is behind him. As if possessed by
the pounding of monsoon rains and moaning of paratroopers
somebody tall and black will rise from the collective memory.

IV

The frame of the extinct sky is empty, emptier than empty. No starlings
or any other birds. No cloudy weavings, no long sleepless walks in
January. Perhaps there is a south breeze, but this is not important.
White frost crackles under somebody's feet. You are at peace, hollowed

to the nerves' end. You are without hatred or envy, you don't care
about the calendar of people in your life. Bare fish bone. — I could
keep talking about your dislike of closed spaces. — You are smooth
as Venetian glass. Silent and dense like water. Water, water. —

Deer are freezing in the forest. Their warm skin, how it breathes
with the concentric circles of dusk! A name, a body, a glance:
impregnated with the American plain. Just think how some foreign
bird sharply cuts the air above the Mohave desert!

V

Honey is dripping from a wild cherry-tree. It used to heal wounds.
Not any longer. — Disappointment grows in somebody's lungs.
Facts follow each other. Not changing anything, of course.
Nor astronomy or tools for anesthesia: nothing is interesting

or exciting anymore. — Afterwards it rained, most likely. —
And he says quietly: I'll disintegrate from stillness.
His widened nostrils aren't catching the smell of ozone and
hatred anymore. Hatred that for everybody else should forever

linger like mists above the melancholic riverbed of the Danube.
An early blooming of a dandelion, yellowing dully in his hands.
And long fields of shamrock, stretched as bodies of war victims.
He will now look around. Whispering inaudibly *gracias a la vida.*

VI

'Then there was whispering in the next-door room. And quiet moaning
of the wooden floor. If you'd glance through the window in this very
moment, you'd see a bus on the narrow empty road. The vein in your
throat would be throbbing faster. Your mouth would be slightly open.

You grew up on the street. The whole world is now asleep. Children and
history as well. Nobody thinks of flying. The volume of memory is
hardening, faces turned toward the wall. Perhaps, in your dreams, they
are being taken to be shot. The next day you dream about a live woman.

Her nude body, etc. etc. You never sing. You could, sometimes at
night, stride into a park and whistle softly. 'Then you'd perhaps
notice the shapes, the sounds, the colors of dreamtime where you
would not die. Over and over again.

VII

The seam in the sky has vanished. The land has sunk in the water.
If there will once be an urgent need to return, there will be no
path left. Into the dark edge of the horizon a warship is framed,
sailing through soldiers' dreams. No person around. No one to ask

about the squeaking of mice, trembling in the air. No one to wonder
why flies are gathering into a swarm. Perhaps this is history for
them. For those who dream all this. Let the flowers wither, buckweat,
linden-tree leaf. Because this morning even the animals don't

rise from their cold shelters. One more sign of fear. Somewhere
above the Hungarian plain sings a nightingale. I think not for long.
A gun-blast will take him out of the image. Once and forever.
As if made of pure carbon seems this dreaming, the heritage of no one.

NOTES ON THE POETS

ALEŠ DEBELJAK (b. 1961) graduated in Comparative Literature from the University of Ljubljana and is now a Ph.D. candidate in Social Thought at Syracuse University in New York. He has published four books of poetry, three of cultural criticism, and edited a book of American short stories. His awards include the Prešeren Prize (the Slovenian National Book Award), and the Hayden Carruth Poetry Prize at Syracuse University. His books of poetry have been translated into Serbo-Croatian, Polish, and Italian, and anthologized in *Double Vision: Four Slovenian Poets* (The Poetry Miscellany Books), 1993, *This Same Sky* (MacMillan, 1992), and *Child of Europe* (Penguin, 1990). In the United States, he published a poetry chapbook, *Chronicle of Melancholy* (1989). He has edited Serbian, Croatian, and Slovenian sections for *Shifting Borders: East European Poetry in the Eighties* (Fairleigh Dickinson University Press, 1993). *Anxious Moments,* his book-length volume of poems in English translation is forthcoming from White Pine Press.

MILAN DEKLEVA (b. 1946) graduated in Comparative Literature from the University of Ljubljana and works as a journalist. His books of poetry include *Mushi mushi* (1971), *Dopisovanja* (Correspondences, 1978), *Nagovarjanja* (Evocations, 1979), *Narečje telesa* (The Body Accent, 1987), *Zapriseženi prah* (Sworn Dust, 1987), *Odjedanje božjega* (Eating-Away of Divine, 1988), and *Anaximander* (1990). He has also published three plays, and two books of poems for children.

NIKO GRAFENAUER (b. 1940) graduated in Comparative Literature from the University of Ljubljana. Formerly a free-lance writer, he is now an editor at the major publishing house, Mladinska Knjiga. In addition, he translates widely from the German and Serbo-Croation. His books of poetry include, *Večer pred praznikom* (An Evening Before Holiday, 1962), *Stiska jezika* (The Anxiety of Language, 1965), *Stukature* (Stucco-Works, 1975), *Palimpsesti* (Palimpsests, 1984), and *Elegije* (Elegies, 1990). In addition, he has published nine books of poems for children, five books of criticism, and edited a number of poetry anthologies. In addition, he has won many awards, and has a book of poems translated into Serbo-Croatian and Macedonian.

173

MAJA HADERLAP (b. 1961) graduated in theater studies from the University of Vienna, Austria. She is the editor of the literary magazine, *Mladje*, in the Carinthia region of Austria, where she makes her home. She has published two collections of poems, *Zalik pesmi* (Nymph Poems, 1986), and *Bajalice* (Spellbound Poems, 1989). She has won several awards, including the Prešeren Prize. In addition, she translates from and into German, and writes criticism, particularly on literature by the Slovenian minority in Austria.

ALOJZ IHAN (b. 1961), an M.D., is a research fellow at the Institute of Microbiology, the University of Ljubljana. In 1991-92, he was a visiting research fellow at the University of Genova, Italy. He has published the following books of poetry: *Srebrnik* (Silver Coin, 1985), *Igralci pokra* (The Poker Players, 1989), and *Selected Poems* (1990), and is included in *Double Vision: Four Slovenian Poets* (1993). The first two books were translated into Serbo-Croatian and Macedonian. He has won numerous literary awards in Slovenia, including the Prešeren Prize in 1985.

MILAN JESIH (b. 1953) studied Comparative Literature at the University of Ljubljana and is now a free lance writer and translator from English and Russian. A prolific and popular author of more than fifteen radio and stage plays, he has published the following books of poems: *Uran v urinu, gospodar* (Urine in Urine, Lord, 1972), *Legende* (Legends, 1974), *Kobalt* (1976), *Volfram* (1980), *Usta* (Mouth, 1985), *Soneti* (Sonnets, 1989).

KAJETAN KOVIČ (b. 1931) graduated in Comparative Literature from the University of Ljubljana. He is Editor-in-Chief of Državna založba Slovenije. He translates poetry from German, French, and Russian, and is a member of the Slovenian Academy of Arts and Sciences. His award-winning books of poetry include, *Pesmi štirih* (Four Poets, 1953, with J. Menart, T. Pavček, and C. Zlobec), *Prezgodnji dan* (Premature Day, 1956), *Korenine vetra* (The Roots of Wind, 1961), *Ogenjvoda* (Firewater, 1965), *Mala čitanka* (A Small Reader, 1973), *Labrador* (1976), and *Dežele* (Lands, 1988). In addition, he has published five books of poetry and fiction for children, two novels, and a book of short stories. His books of poems are translated into Serbo-Croatian, Macedonian, and German.

EDVARD KOCBEK (1904-1981) studied theology in Maribor, and Romance languages in Berlin, Lyon, and Paris, and graduated in Slavic literatures from the University of Ljubljana. The leading Christian Socialist intellectual, he was a founding member of the Liberation Front in 1941 and was in partisan leadership. After the war, he was a vice-president of the Slovenian government and a minister in the Yugoslavian government. He fell out of grace with the communists in 1952 and withdrew from politics. He translated extensively from both French and German. His books of poetry include *Zemlja* (Soil, 1934), *Groza* (Horror, 1963), *Poročilo* (Report, 1969), and *Žerjavica* (Glow, 1974). He has also published five important war journals and three books of non-fiction. His books have been translated into French andGerman. A book of poems in English translation is, *At the Door of Evening*, Muses Co, Quebec, 1991.

v

SVETLANA MAKAROVIC (b. 1939) graduated in stage-acting from the University of Ljubljana and makes her living as a free-lance writer and as a singer-songwriter. She has published the following books of poetry: *Somrak* (Twilight, 1964), *Kresna noč* (Mid-Summer's Night, 1968), *Volčje jagode* (Wolf's Berries, 1972), *Srceved* (Heart Stuff, 1973), *Pelin žena* (Poison Woman, 1978), *Sosed Gora* (Neighbor Mountain, 1980), and *Pesmi o Sloveniji* (Poems on Slovenia, 1984). She is also a popular and prolific writer for children, with fifteen books and two plays to her credit.

BORIS A. NOVAK (b. 1953) graduated in Comparative Literature from the University of Ljubljana. He was an IREX visiting scholar in theater studies at the University of Minnesota-Minneapolis in 1989, and American Bank Visiting Professor of Humanities at the University of Tennessee-Chattanooga in 1991. He has won many awards, including the Prešeren Prize. He works as an editor and translates from English and French. His book of poetry include *Stihožitje* (Still-Life-In-Verse, 1977), *Hči spomina* (Daughter of Memory, 1981), *1001 stih* (1001 Verses, 1983), and *Kronanje* (Coronation, 1984). He has also published many poetry books and plays for children. His chapbook, *Coronation*, was published in the United States in 1990.

JURE POTOKAR (b. 1956) studied Slavic literatures at the University of Ljubljana. He works as a music editor and as a translator in Ljubljana. *Aiton* (1980), *Pokrajina se tu nagiba proti jugu* (The Landscape Here Bends Toward the South, 1982), *Ambienti zvočnih pokrajin* (The Ambients of

175

Sonic Landscapes, 1986), *Stvari v praznini* (Things in the Void, 1990) are among his books of poetry. He has won numerous awards, including the Prešeren Prize in 1986 and has a book of poems translated into Serbo-Croatian.He has work included in *Double Vision: Four Slovenian Poets* (1993), and a number of book translations from English to his credit, including sections in an authoritative *Anthology of American Poetry in the 20th Century.*

GREGOR STRNISA (1930-1987) was imprisoned, as a teenager, by the communists in the wake of the war. He graduated in English and German literature from the University of Ljubljana. He worked free-lance and received numerous awards, including the Prešeren Prize. His books of poetry include *Mozaiki* (Mosaics, 1959), *Odisej* (Odyssey, 1963), *Zvezde* (Stars, 1965), *Želod* (Acorn, 1972), *Mirabilia* (1973), *Oko* (Eye, 1974), *Jajce* (Egg, 1975), *Škarje* (Scissors, 1975, and *Vesolje* (Universe, 1983). In addition, he has published three books of fiction for children and four poetic plays.

IVO SVETINA (b. 1948) graduated in Comparative Literature from the University of Ljubljana. He worked at the National TV Network and is now a director of the Youth Theater in Ljubljana. His books of poetry include *Plovi na jagodi pupa magnolija do zlatih vladnih palač* (Float on the Strawberry, a Doll of Magnolia, to the Golden Governmental Palaces, 1971), *Heliks in Tibija* (Helix and Tibia, 1972), *Botticelli,* 1975, *Vaša partijska ljubezen, očetje!* (Your Party Love, Fathers!, 1976), *Joni* (1976), *Dissertationes,* 1977, *Bulbul,* 1982, *Marija in živali* (Mary and the Animals, 1986), *Peti Rokopisi* (Singing Manuscripts, 1987), *Tibet,* 1990, and *Almagest,* 1991.

TOMAZ SALAMUN (b. 1941) graduated in Art History from the University of Ljubljana. As a member of the avant-garde group OHO he exhibited world-wide, including at the Museum of Modern Art in New York. In 1971-73 he was a member of the International Writing Program at the University of Iowa and was a writing fellow at Yaddo and MacDowell, as well as a visiting Fulbright poet at Columbia University. He has published over twenty books of poetry in Slovenia and won many awards, including the Prešeren Prize. His poetry books have been translated into German, Serbo-Croatian, Swedish, and Polish. In addition to two chapbooks, his *Selected Poems* (Ecco Press, 1988) and

176

The Shepherd, The Hunter (Pedernal Press, 1992) appeared in English translation.

VENO TAUFER (b. 1933) graduated in Comparative Literature from the University of Ljubljana. He worked as a journalist for the Radio Ljubljana and BBC, London, and was a visiting Fulbright poet at the University of Maryland. He now works for the Ministry of Foreign Affairs. He translates from English, Russian, and Serbo-Croatian. His books of poems include *Svinčene zvezde* (Lead Stars, 1958), *Jetnik prostosti* (A Prisoner of Freedom, 1963), *Vaje in naloge* (Excercises and Assignments, 1969), *Podatki* (Data, 1972), *Prigode* (Happenings, 1973), *Pesmarica rabljenih besed* (A Song-Book of Used Words, 1975), *Ravnanje žebljev in druge pesmi* (Strengthening the Nails and Other Poems, 1979), *Sonetje* (Sonnets, 1979), *Tercine za obtolčeno trobento* (Terzac-rimac for the Bruised Trumpet, 1985), *Vodenjaki* (Water People, 1986), and *Črepinje pesmi* (Shards of a Poem, 1990). In addition, he has published two books of theater criticism and a play. *New Music* (1990) is a chapbook of his poetry in English translation.

JOŽE UDOVIČ (1912-1986) graduated in Slavic literatures from the University of Ljubljana. During the war, he was in an Italian concentration camp, and from 1943 in the partisan movement. After the war, he was a prolific translator of poetry and fiction from French, German, English, Russian, and Spanish. He was a member of the Slovenian Academy of Arts and Sciences. His books of poems include *Ogledalo sanj* (A Mirror of Dreams, 1961), *Darovi* (Gifts, 1975), and *Oko in senca* (The Eye and the Shadow, 1982). He has also published a book of his journals.

DANE ZAJC (b. 1929) graduated from a secondary school in Ljubljana, where he now works as a librarian. He was a Fulbright poet at Columbia University, and is now President of the Slovenian Writers Association. He has won all the major literary awards, including the Prešeren Prize. His book of poetry include *Požgana trava* (Burned Grass, 1958), *Jezik iz zemlje* (A Tongue of Soil, 1961), *Ubijavci kač* (Snake Killers, 1968), *Rozengruntar* (1975), *Si videl* (Did You See, 1979), *Zarotitve* (Incantations, 1985), and *Zbrana dela* (Collected Works, 1991). In addition to numerous selections of his poems, he has published five plays, and four books of poetry for children. His poetry has been translated into Serbo-Croatian, Macedonian, and German. In the United States, he has published a chapbook of poems, *Ashes* (1990).

177

MICHAEL BIGGINS is a Slavic Collection Librarian at the University of Kansas, Lawrence, where he received his Ph.D. in Russian and Slavic Studies. He has taught at Middlebury College and Knox College. His translations of Slovenian poetry have appeared in *Partisan Review, Ploughshares,* and *New England Review/Bread Loaf Quarterly.* He has contributed translations to *Double Vision: Four Slovenian Poets* (1993), and his translation of Boris Pahor's novel, *Nekropolis* was published by Harcourt Brace Jovanovic in 1993.

MILNE HOLTON received his Ph.D. from Yale University and teaches English and American literature at the University of Maryland. He translates from Serbian, Slovenian, Macedonian, Polish, and German. He received a translation grant from the National Endowment for the Humanities and was a visiting Fulbright scholar to Macedonia and Sweden. He has published seven books of translation and criticism, including *Serbian Poetry from the Beginnings to the Present* (ed. & translator with Vasa D. Michailovich), 1989; *Austrian Poetry Today* (ed. & translator with Herbert Kuhner), 1985; *Reading the Ashes: An Anthology of the Poetry of Modern Macedonia* (ed. & translator with Graham W. Ried), 1977.

RICHARD JACKSON has published three collections of poems, *Part of the Story, Worlds Apart,* and *Alive All Day* (Cleveland State Poetry Center, 1992), and two books of criticism, *The Dismanteling of Time in Contemporary Poetry,* and *Acts of Mind: Conversations with Contemporary American Poets.* He has edited *Double Vision: Four Slovenian Poets* (The Poetry Miscellany Books, 1993) and has been a Fulbright poet to former Yugoslavia and has extensively traveled in Slovenia. He has won the Agee Prize, Pushcart Prize, NEH and NEA fellowships. He teaches in the Vermont College MFA Program and at the University of Tennessee-Chattanooga where he edits *The Poetry Miscellany.*

SONJA KRAVANJA graduated in comparative literature at the University of Ljubljana. She was an IREX Visiting Scholar at the University of Colorado-Boulder and has received two translation fellowships from the Witter Bynner Foundation for Poetry. She is the translator of *The Dictionary of Silence,* by Aleš Debeljak, and *The*

Shepherd, The Hunter: Selected Poems of Tomaž Šalamun,((Pedernal Press, 1992) which was awarded the 1993 Translation Center Merit Award from the Translation Center of Columbia University. She lives in Santa Fe, New Mexico.

JOŽE LAZAR was educated in Trieste, Italy, at the University of Ljubljana, and at the University of British Columbia. He has published numerous translations of Slovenian poetry in literary magazines in the United States, Canada, and Australia, in additional to a substantial body of essays.

TOM LOZAR came from his native Ljubljana, Slovenia to Canada at the age of eight. He received a Ph.D. in American Literature from the University of Toronto and teaches in the Department of English at Vainer College, Montreal. He is the translator of a book of selected poems by Edvard Kocbek, *Na vratih zvečer/At the Door at Evening* (Muses & Co., 1990) and has contributed translation to *Double Vision: Four Slovenian Poets* (The Poetry Miscellany Books, 1993).

CHRISTOPHER MERRILL is the author of two collections of poetry, *Workbook* and *Fevers & Tides;* co-translator of *Constellations* by André Breton, and *Slow Down Construction* by Breton, René Char, and Paul Eluard; and editor of *Outcroppings: John McPhee in the West* and, most recently, *The Forgotten Language: Contemporary Poets and Nature* (Peregrine Smith, 1991). He has contributed translations to *Double Vision: Four Slovenian Poets* (The Poetry Miscellany Books, 1993), and has a non-fiction book on the culture and politics of former Yugoslavia forthcoming from Henry Holt.

LILI POTPARA graduated in English Translation Workshop from the University of Ljubljana and has translated a number of Slovenian works into English including short stories by Drago Jančar in *The Day Tito Died: Contemporary Slovenian Short Stories* (Forest Books: London 1993).

TOM PRIESTLY received his Ph.D. in Slavic Studies from Simon Fraser University. He teaches in the Department of Slavic and East European Studies, University of Alberta, Edmonton, Canada. He is a co-author of *Reading Rules for Russian* (1980). His other publications focus on Russian Linguistics and Slovenian dialectics of the Carintia region of Austria. He translates prose and poetry from Russian and Slovene and is editor-in-chief of *Slovene Studies.*

MICHAEL SCAMMELL has translated novels by Tolstoy, Dostoevsky, Nabokov, and Fedin from Russian, and poems by several poets from Croatia and Slovenia. He was co-editor (with Veno Taufer) of a special issue of *Modern Poetry in Translation* devoted to Slovenia in 1970, and his translations have appeared in *New Writing in Yugoslavia* (Penguin Books, 1970), and *Contemporary Yugoslav Poetry* (University of Iowa Press, 1977). He and Veno Taufer are currently preparing *The Selected Poems of Edvard Kocbek.* The author of the highly acclaimed *Solzhenitsyn: A Biography* (W.W. Norton, 1984), he teaches at Cornell University in Ithaca, New York.

JOŽE ŽOHAR came from his native Slovenia to Australia as a child. He settled in New South Wales and held various jobs before he started editing a Slovenian-Australian literary magazine. A part-time radio producer, he is the author of *Aurora Australis,* a collection of poems.